DISCOVER
STOCKHOLM

ALL YEAR ROUND

D1380065

STOCKHOLM
INFORMATION
SERVICE
CONVENTION & VISITORS BUREAU

SVENSKA
TURISTFÖRENINGEN

DISCOVER STOCKHOLM ALL YEAR ROUND
is produced by the Swedish Touring Club (STF), Publications Department,
in association with the Stockholm Information Service (SIS).

MANAGING EDITOR: Hans Bauer.

EDITORIAL BOARD: Ulf Johansson and Eva Nyströmer (STF),
Mats Wåhlin and Roland Berndt (SIS), Erling Matz.

The sections on the Stockholm archipelago,
the Lake Mälaren district and restaurants were written by
Erling Matz. All other sections were written by Hans Bauer.

EDITOR, ENGLISH VERSION: Richard Cadwalader, WireWorks AB

GRAPHIC DESIGN: Gunnar Palmgren.

COVER PICTURES: Front: Norr Mälarstrand and the City Hall,
Kaknäs Tower in the background. Photo: Claes Löfgren/Pressens Bild
Back: Skeppsbron and Gamla Stan as seen from the heights
of Södermalm. Photo: Hans Nelsäter/Bildarkivet

© Swedish Touring Club & Stockholm Information Service

REPRODUCTION AND PRINTING: Fälths Tryckeri AB, Värnamo 1996

STF Publication no.: 3179

ISBN 91-7156-148-X

Contents

Welcome to Stockholm. Photo: Hans Nelsäter/ Bildarkivet

Carl Milles's statue "Gud Fader på Himmelsbågen" on Nacka Strand, greets all visitors entering Stockholm by boat. Photo: Bo Dahlin/Bildhuset

A NATURAL METROPOLIS

Stockholm has everything
a big city should have: exciting shops,
theatres, museums, cafés, nightclubs and restaurants.
Yet, for a large city, Stockholm is also quite unusual.
It's possible to swim in the middle of town; to catch salmon,
sea trout and perch from the quays; to look at wild birds
of prey and deer in the large parks; to take off
in a hot-air balloon; or even to rent a canoe
and explore the city from the water.

In contrast to many other large cities, Stockholm, with more than a million inhabitants, is not situated by a river. Nor is it situated, like Madrid, Mexico City or Johannesburg, high up in the middle of the country.

Stockholm is, quite simply, a number of inhabited islands and beaches between two great stretches of water – to the east the Baltic Sea and to the west Mälaren, Sweden's third largest lake.

The only part of the town centre on the mainland is that to the north of the city. The rest is on 14 islands. So it's with good reason that Stockholm proclaims itself "a city on the water".

The water and its many parks make Stockholm a city within nature rather than one that has taken nature over. Of course, humans have interfered, at times violently, to shape it. Yet nature's presence is felt everywhere. Of Stockholm's total area, 190 square kilometres, one-third consists of the built-up area, one-third is water and one-third is parks and green areas.

An excellent way to experience Stockholm from the water is to take one of the sightseeing boats which leave from Norrström, right beside Kungsträdgården (the King's Garden), or from Klara Mälarstrand at the Stadshuset (City Hall).

Seeing the City

Of course, as is true of many other big cities, the best way to experience Stockholm is by foot.

If you don't get lost among the shops or in the narrow streets of Gamla Stan (the Old Town), it takes only about half an hour to walk from Kungsträdgården, in the middle of the city, through the Old Town and past Slussen (the Sluice Gate) to Södermalmstorg (Södermalm Square).

There you will find the 100-year-old yet still modern Katarinahissen (Katarina Lift), which takes you up to the Mosebacke Torg at the top of the cliffs of the Söder hills. At the yellow building, Södra Teatern (Södra

Stockholm is situated on two large bodies of water, the Baltic Sea and Lake Mälaren. In the foreground one can see southern Djurgården and the Nordic Museum, in the background is the Palace and the City Hall. Uppermost in the picture one can see Södermalm to the left and the Västerbron (first bridge) and Essingleden (second bridge) over Lake Mälaren to the right. Photo: Hans Nelsäter/Bildarkivet

Theatre), there is a gateway and a stairway leading up to a terrace, Mosebacketerrassen. The view of Stockholm from that terrace, where you can eat and drink outside in the summer, is something to remember.

There are any number of other places to view the city from on high. Kaknästornet (Kaknäs Tower) on Djurgården is the tallest and most impressive. The view from the Stadshus tower is magnificent, and the same can be said of another high brick tower, Bredablick (Broad View) at Skansen. But it is perhaps Mosebacke that offers the most exciting and direct views.

From here the town extends outwards. Church towers mingle with eaves, famous buildings with whole town districts. The traffic can be heard from Stadsgårdskajen, a faint and monotonous hum. Down on Strömmen (the stream), the Djurgårds ferry leaves the Old Town for Djurgården, whilst nearby chaffinches and sparrows chirp merrily away.

Historic Ground

Chaffinches and sparrows? It was from Mosebacketerrassen that August Strindberg derived his inspiration for the opening lines of *Röda Rummet* (The Red Room), the novel which created such a stir when it appeared in

---

Bellman's Proud Town

Wenches and nymphs, tipplers and troublemakers. Carl Michael Bellman's way of writing verse about life in Stockholm in the second half of the 18th century made him one of Sweden's greatest and most loved poets. Many of Bellman's *Fredmans Epistles* were created in two rooms at Urvädersgränd 3. His literary figures were often based on characters from real life: Father Mowitz, Corporal Mollberg, the clockmaker Fredman and the beautiful Ulla Winblad. To visit the Bellman Museum at Stora Henriksvik on Långholmen, ring ☎ 08-669 69 69 for information.

Carl Michael Bellman (1740–1795). Photo: Pressens Bild

View of Stockholm from Ersta as seen by Elias Martin in the 1790s. Water coloured contour study. Photo: Francis Bruun/Stockholms Stadsmuseum

1879. Apart from the chaffinches and sparrows in the opening lines, it depicts the life of Stockholm bohemians of that time. With its impressionistic style, it is regarded as Sweden's first modern novel.

Walking from Kungsträdgården to Mosebacketerrassen, you'll wander from hip "in" places like the Café Opera and the small outdoor restaurants in Kungsträdgården across Helgeandsholmen and in through the Old Town's striking mixture of contemporary commerce and historic sites. Västerlånggatan, the street with the most shops, runs approximately above the wall which encircled the town in the 13th century.

Seven hundred years ago the water was two metres higher than it is today, and the shore was just below Västerlånggatan and Österlånggatan (West and East Long Street). Stockholm then had 1000 inhabitants, most of whom made their living as craftsworkers or traders. You can get a glimpse of life in those days by visiting the Medeltidsmuseet (Museum of the Medieval Stockholm) on Helgeandsholmen.

Towards the Hills of Söder

At ground level, or more correctly water level, in Slussen is the Karl Johan sluice. It was named after the first Bernadotte king, Karl XIV Johan, who reigned from 1818 to 1844. He can be seen proudly riding his bronze horse right beside Slussen. The Katarinahissen was a great success when it was inaugurated in March 1883. At that time it cost 5 öre to go up and 3 to come back down again. Over one and a half million people, both Stockholmers and tourists, were captivated by this masterpiece of technology, comparable to an airplane ride. When Slussen was rebuilt in the 1930s, the old lift was pulled down and replaced by the present one, designed in the then-prevalent functionalist style.

The view from Mosebacketerrassen is more obscured now than when Arvid Falk, the protagonist in *Röda Rummet,* shook his fist and challenged the town. Even so, it's easy to get an idea of the diverse characters of Stockholm: Söder with its history as a working-class district, the Old Town, Kungsholmen and the City Hall, and the Hötorgskrapor (the skyscrapers near Hötorget).

Recognisable Places

The round cupolas of Hedvig Eleonoras church appear behind the National Museum, which is on Blasieholmen. The church, which dates from the 17th century, is in Östermalm. Further to the right, on Djurgården, you have the large Nordiska museet (Nordic Museum) with the Vasamuseet (Vasa Museum) in the foreground. Easiest of all to recognise, however, is Gröna Lund (the amusement park) – you can't miss the rollercoaster tracks. Behind Gröna Lund is Skansen, with buildings of cultural and historic interest from all over Sweden, plus an outstanding zoo featuring everything from seals and elks to crocodiles and lemurs.

Of course, opinions vary on what is most interesting to explore. But one district that just can't be missed is the area around Kungsträdgården. So follow along and stroll among the crowds in the city.

*Stockholm's City Hall seen from Riddarfjärden. Photo: Ingmar Karlsson/
Pressens Bild*

The City Hall

Scientists and writers all over the world share a common dream: to be invited to a party at the City Hall on 10 December. It's on that evening that Blå Hallen (the Blue Hall) is turned into a party room for that year's Nobel Prize winners. Nobel Prize winner or not, everybody is welcome to the showings of the Golden Room, the Council Room, the Prince's Gallery, Blå Hallen and Carl Milles's statues outside the building. From May to September you can enjoy the view from the tower Tre Kronor (Three Crowns), open 10.00–15.00. The City Hall was inaugurated on Midsummer Day 1923, exactly 400 years after Gustav Vasa marched into the town for his coronation. The architect was Ragnar Östberg.

The Central City

*Boutiques and stores, theatres and cinemas,
restaurants and cafés. Everyone and everything gathers
in the heart of the city – urbanites and country bumpkins,
tourists, Swedes and foreigners.*

On a fine summer's evening in Kungsträdgården (the King's Garden)
you get a good idea of everyday Stockholm life. People move about, sitting, standing or lying in the small but much loved rectangular park in
the middle of town. The sounds of Chilean pan players mix with those of
reggae from a cassette player somewhere on the lawns. Children play,
whilst boules and chess players concentrate on their games. Kungsträdgården is also situated adjacent to Stockholm's principle tourist bureau, the Tourist Centre in Sverigehuset.

"Kungsan", as the garden is known, dates back to the 15th century. In
those days it was the royal court's "cabbage yard" – in other words, fruit
and vegetables were grown here. Since then its role and appearance have
changed, and it is now used both as a splendid court garden and as a parade ground.

Of course, the city is not just about amusement. Thousands of people
travel there daily to work. Many of the
country's banks have their headquarters there, and many political offices
are based in the city. The government
chancellery, Rosenbad, is near Tegel-
backen, and ministries are in the vicinity.

Skating in Kungsträdgården.
Photo: Hans Nelsäter/Bildarkivet

The Royal Opera is a popular destination for many Stockholmers interested in the performing arts. Photo: Hans T. Dahlskog/Pressens Bild

The Foreign Office (Utrikesdepartementet) at Gustav Adolfs Torg has a fine façade in the French classical style. Above the entrance, written in gold, are the words "Sophia Albertina". She was the sister of Gustav III and lived there towards the end of the 18th century. The princess had the façade rebuilt in order to make it as fine as the one on the Opera just opposite.

The original Opera no longer exists. That Sophia's brother was assassinated there at a masked ball in 1792 actually has nothing to do with the disappearance of the Opera. What happened was that the Foreign Office's twin building was pulled down a hundred years later, to be replaced by today's Opera.

On the Kungsträdgården side of the Opera is the gourmet restaurant Operakällaren (the Opera Cellar) and Café Opera. "The Café" (no further specification is necessary to Stockholmers) has maintained its position as the place to be in Stockholm for some 15 years. It's still a good place for bumping into celebrities now and again.

But you're likely to find the biggest crowds on Drottninggatan. This is

Colourful Easter decorations being sold at Hötorget. Photo: Jeppe Wikström/ Pressens Bild

A Southern Square

Hötorget has always been associated with a market. During the 16th century the farmers from Roslagen (the area north-east of Stockholm) sold hay and straw there. Around the turn of the century the "Torgmadamer" (madams of the square) came to sell Christmas trees, Shrovetide whips made of birch twigs, fruit or whatever the season demanded and offered. There is a southern atmosphere here; Stockholmers enjoy the spring and summer sunshine sitting on the steps of the Konserthuset (Concert Hall), where you can see one of sculptor Carl Milles's masterpieces, *Orpheus*. The steps and the square are both natural meeting places, just as the architect Ivar Tengbom planned in his 1926 design. Another popular meeting place in Hötorget is the recently completed Filmstaden Sergel cinema complex.

the street that runs in a north-westerly direction from Strömmen and Rosenbad past Sergels Torg and the Åhléns department store up to the observatory in Vasastan. Drottninggatan is often full of Stockholmers out shopping or simply walking about. Most of it is a pedestrian precinct, where street vendors (illegally) display their goods on rugs. There is an explanation for the rugs: when the police walk by, the vendors can quickly roll up their goods and move along; the instant the police have passed, they roll out their rugs and commerce begins again.

Having mentioned Åhléns, we ought to put in a word for the NK department store. NK is perhaps Sweden's most exclusive shopping center and is to be found on Hamngatan. It was inaugurated in 1915 after the then-fashionable architect Ferdinand Boberg had been to the United States and seen what "real" stores should look like. NK is divided into a number of different shops, and each retailer rents a section of the shop floor; this arrangement is hardly perceptible to the customer.

Shops, shops. Stureplan has once again become one of the most popular sections of town, both for shopping and other diversions. So much so that it nearly matches its reputation from the 1930s, '40s and '50s when Stureplan was the number one meeting place.

Queen Kristina, painted by David Beck (1650). Photo: Bengt Eurenius/ Pressens Bild

The Enigmatic Queen

Kristina was a woman of contrasts. She became queen in 1633, aged only 6, shortly after her father, Gustav II Adolf, died in the mists on the battlefield at Lutzen. She thanked God for having made her a woman. Yet at the same time she despised women and socialised only with men. One minute she was cursing like a stevedore, the next rubbing shoulders with Europe's most renowned philosophers. Such a woman did not feel at home in the Lutheran world. In 1654 she abdicated and soon thereafter gave up the religion her father had fought so hard for. She became a Roman Catholic and settled in Rome. "The heretic's daughter" is buried in St Peter's. Drottninggatan is named after her.

The Old Town

A walk in Gamla Stan (the Old Town)
is comparable to a walk through Stockholm's past
from the 13th to the 18th century. Streets that date
from the Middle Ages lead to palaces and squares
built in the 17th century, a period during which
Sweden enjoyed great power.

The Royal Palace is the most prominent building in Gamla Stan and holds a special place among the royal palaces of the world, not so much for its size and beauty but because it is open to the public. See page 94.

The first royal family to move into the palace was that of Gustav III, then-crown prince, together with his brother and sisters, father Adolf Fredrik and mother Lovisa Ulrika, in 1754. At that time, rococo style was all the rage at court. Decorating the castle was a task which gathered together an eclectic group of top artists of the day, namely Carl Hårleman, Jean Eric Rehn and Louis Masreliez. The construction of the palace provided them with the opportunity to create the combination of rococo and Gustavian style for which Sweden is now famous. The elements of this style spread, first to the wealthy bourgeoisie and then out into the country. Without the palace, Sweden wouldn't look the way it does today.

Writers and Artists

Stockholm's stock exchange is on Stortorget (Main Square). Designed by Erik Palmstedt during the early years of the reign of Gustav III, the building is regarded as one of the city's finest. The Swedish Academy was one

Västerlånggatan in Gamla Stan is a busy street with many shops. Here one can buy clothing, look into artisans' workshops, visit galleries or get a bite to eat. Photo: Hans T. Dahlskog/Pressens Bild

HOTELS,
HOSTELS AND
CAMPING

Hotels

*There are hundreds of hotels in Stockholm,
and the prices naturally range greatly, from simple single rooms
with a shower and toilet in the corridor to large suites with
a private lift and a view of the palace.*

The Hotellcentralen is of great use when booking both hotel rooms and hostels. It is Stockholm's official accommodation agency and is run by the Stockholm Information Service (SIS. It is at the Central Station, making it easy for you, whether you arrive by train or by plane (airport buses stop at the Central Station).

Hotellcentralen helps you with free advance bookings of rooms at the majority of hotels in Stockholm. You can even get help with tickets for sightseeing boats; buying a Stockholm Travel Card and a Tourist Card (see page 146 and 148); and bookings of Weekendpaketet in, for example, the archipelago or the Mälaren countryside. Direct booking over the counter costs 40 kronor for hotels and 15 for hostels.

Hotellcentralen, Central Station, 111 20 Stockholm ☎ 08-24 08 80, fax 08-791 86 66. It is even possible to book hotels through Stockholm Today, e-mail: hotels@stoinfo.se.

Swedish Touring Club Hostels

Staying in a Youth Hostel is an excellent and affordable lodging alternative. The Swedish Touring Club's Stockholm hostels cost only 90–140 SEK per night for members. Non-members pay an additional 35 SEK.

Central Stockholm

af Chapman
Västra Brobänken,
Skeppsholmen
☎ 08-679 50 15
Open: Year round

The white full-rigger which defied stormy seas until 1939 is now one of Stockholm's distinctive town symbols and a very attractive hostel. Bookings ought to be made well in advance. Stay in 2–10-bed cabins (women's and men's sections only). In summer, breakfast is served on deck. For those coming by car, please note that parking is strictly limited.

Skeppsholmen
Västra Brobänken,
Skeppsholmen
☎ 08-679 50 17
Open: Year round

This hostel with a little over 150 beds is beside af Chapman. Stay in rooms with 2–4 beds or at an even lower price in large accommodations. There are also four rooms for handicapped people. Breakfast on board af Chapman. Extremely limited parking.

Previous pages: "The world's loveliest youth hostel." Swedish Touring Club's ship af Chapman. Photo: Hans Nelsäter/Bildarkivet

The Grand Hôtel is Stockholm's most fashionable. It is located along Strömkajen where the archipelago boats come and go. Photo: Jeppe Wikström/Pressens Bild

Life is calm in Långholmen Jail now that the criminals have moved out and a youth hostel has moved in. Photo: Svenska Turistföreningen

Långholmen
Långholmen
☎ 08-668 05 10
Open: Year round

The old prison on Långholmen has been Stockholm's largest hostel since 1989 with 254 beds. Stay in rooms with 2–5 beds, all nonsmoking. Ten rooms/23 beds are for handicapped people. Amenities include a laundry room, restaurant, Prison bar and café. Plenty of parking.

Zinkensdamm
Zinkens väg 20
☎ 08-616 81 00
Open: Year round

With 464 beds in summer and 202 in winter, Zinkensdamm's hostel on Söder is one of the largest. It is at the colony plots in Tantolunden. Stay in rooms with 2–4 beds. Selfcatering breakfast, cafeteria, washing machine. Limited but free parking, weekends and nights.

Stockholm County

Adelsö
Adelsögården, Ekerö
☎ 08-560 514 50
Open: 15/6–31/8

This hostel accommodates 30 guests in a fine country setting on Adelsö in Mälaren. There is a swimming area with a pier, and canoe and cycle rentals are available. Bus or boat to Stockholm. Stay in rooms with 3 or 4 beds. Self-catering, restaurant and kiosk.

Bosön
Bosön, Lidingö
☎ 08-605 66 05, -06
Open: 19/6–13/8 (closed Midsummer weekend)

Near the National Sport Association's training centre, this hostel accommodates 26 guests. Sports enthusiasts will find most of what they're looking for here: swimming pool, tennis courts, wind surfing, canoes, workout gyms, sauna and more. Stay in rooms with 2 beds. All meals available. Cafeteria. Washing machine.

Huddinge
Sundby Gård,
Sundbygårdsvägen, Huddinge
☎ 08-746 94 80
Open: Year round, 18/8–22/6
groups only

This hostel is south of Stockholm at Orlången Lake, formerly a large workers' house for the Sundby estate. Stay in rooms with 2–6 beds. Self-catering, breakfast, café. Boat hire, lighted trails and fishing. Plenty of parking.

Hågelby
Hågelby Gård, Botkyrka
☎ 08-530 620 20
Open: Year round, 10/8–7/6 by prior reservation

Stay in one of Sweden's most beautiful parks on the shores of Aspen Lake. The Hostel has 28 beds, and guests are accommodated in rooms with 2–6 beds. Self-catering, breakfast and café. Dancing on selected evenings in summer. Playground, ceramics workshop and axe museum.

The Hågelby youth hostel is situated in Botkyrka's Hågelby Park, one of Sweden's finest folk parks. Photo: Svenska Turistföreningen

Hökarängen

Martinskolan, Munstycksvägen
18, Hökarängen
☎ 08-94 17 65
Open: 24/6–11/8

When the students at the Waldorf
School go off for their summer
holidays, the hostel guests move
in, 46 in all. Stay in rooms with
2–4 beds. Self-catering, breakfast.
Ten minute walk from underground station. Exercise loop
nearby. Swimming two kilometres. Free parking.

Norrtälje

Brännäsgården, Bältartorps-
gatan 6, Norrtälje
☎ 0176-715 69
Open: 10/6–18/8

Central yet pleasant site in
Norrtälje, the "pearl of Roslagen".
Stay in rooms with 3–6 beds,
self-catering, breakfast, cafeteria.
You can go on tours of the
archipelago from Norrtälje.

Nynäshamn

Nickstagården, Nickstabads-
vägen 17, Nynäshamn
☎ 08-520 208 34
Open: Year round, pre-booking
1/9–31/5

Nickstabadet is on the outskirts
of Nynäshamn, yet not more

than 700 metres from the commuter railway station to Stockholm.
Stay in rooms with 3–4 beds. Self-
catering. Swimming and fishing.
Water slide and mini-golf near the
hostel.

Sigtuna

Kyrkans utbildningscentrum,
Manfred Björquists allé 12,
Sigtuna
☎ 08-592 584 78
Open: 19/6–11/8

This adult education school,
north of Stockholm by Mälaren,
is just outside idyllic Sigtuna. Two
student houses are made into
hostels during the summer. Stay
in rooms with 2–4 beds. Self-
catering, breakfast. Swimming,
fishing, 18-hole golf course,
tennis and more.

Sånga Säby

Faringsö, Svartsjö
☎ 08-560 480 00
Open: 21/6–10/8

A 40-bed hostel on the shores of
Lake Mälaren. Rooms are
furnished with 1–4 beds. Self-
catering, breakfast and occasional
lunches and dinners. Boat
docking. Bathing beach with dock.
Bicycle, canoe and boat rentals.
Trail riding on Icelandic horses.

Södertälje

Tvetagården, Södertälje
☎ 08-550 980 25, 21/8–21/6
550 984 70
Open: Year round (closed 19/12–7/1)

This hostel with space for 60 guests is on the outskirts of Södertälje at Lake Måsnaren. Stay in rooms with 2–6 beds. Self-catering. Swimming, fishing, canoe rental, running track and sport area with sauna by the hostel. Near Sörmlandsleden (Sörmlands Way footpath).

Tyresö

Lilla tyresö, Kyrkvägen 3, Tyresö
☎ 08-770 03 04
Open: 1/6–25/9

Live like a prince in Prince Eugen's summer house adjacent to Tyresö Palace. Bedrooms with 2–4 beds. Self-catering, breakfast and coffee served. Canoeing routes pass by the area. Bicycle rentals. Visitors can take walks in the beautiful forests of the Tyresta National Park.

Upplands-Bro

Säbyholms naturbruks-gymnasium, Bro
☎ 08-582 424 81
Open: 12/6–11/8

Hostel in a park area with capacity for 40 visitors in 2-bed rooms. Self-catering. Washing machine. Gym and running track one kilometre.

Stockholm Archipelago and Roslagen

Arholma

Bull-Augusts Gård, Arholma 162,

Bull-Augusts Gård on Arholma in the northern archipelago. Photo: STF

Björkö
☎ 0176-560 18, booking in advance is required
Open: Year round

Arholma is a classic archipelago island, northeast of Norrtälje. Travel by supply boat from Simpnäs or by the archipelago boat Sjöbris from Nybrokajen in Stockholm. Stay in rooms with 1–6 beds. Self-catering. Note that Arholma is in a military protection zone and that permission for foreign visitors is needed.

Smådalarö
Smådalarö Gård, Dalarö
☎ 08-501 530 73

Open: Year round

This hostel with space for 40 guests lies by Jungfru Bay and close to Smådalarö Manor. Stay in rooms with 4–6 beds. Shower and toilet in all rooms. All meals available. Bathing beach.

Finnhamn
Finnhamns friluftsområde, Ingmarsö
☎ 08-542 462 12, booking in advance necessary
Open: Year round

An old merchant villa in the archipelago, this hostel has space for 76 guests. Go by boat from Stockholm. Stay in rooms with

An old merchant's villa on Finnhamn is now a youth hostel. Photo: Svenska Turistföreningen

2–4 beds, or annexe cottages with 4 beds. Self-catering. Fishing, swimming, boat rental. Restaurant open in summer. Finnhamn is by a boat "trail".

Fjärdlång
Fjärdlång, Dalarö
☎ 08-501 560 92, booking in advance necessary, Hanige Cultural and Recreational Administration, 136 81 Hanige
Open: 10/6–20/8

This hostel, called Thielska villan, is on an island in the southern Stockholm archipelago. Daily connections by boat from Dalarö and Stockholm. Stay in rooms with 2, 4 or 6 beds, in the villa or in cottages. Self-catering. Day trips to Utö, Kymmendö, Dalarö and Huvudskär.

Gällnö
Gällnö, Gällnö village. Advance booking only in writing
☎ 08-571 661 17
Open: 1/5–30/9

A newly renovated hostel in Stockholm's middle archipelago with space for 31 guests. Boat from Stockholm or Sollenkroka. Stay in rooms with 2–6 beds, or 4-bed cottages with pantry. Self-catering, shower and sauna.

Kapellskär
Kapellskär, Riddersholm
☎ 0176-441 69
Open: Year round, 15/8–1/6 reservations required

In a beautiful setting, one kilometre from Viking Lines ferry terminal for Åland/Finland, this hostel has space for 34 guests. Go by boat or bus from Stockholm. Stay in rooms with 3–6 beds. Rambling paths, boat and cycle rental.

Lillsved
Gymnatik- och Idrottsfolkhög-skolan. Lillsved, Värmdö
☎ 08-541 385 30
Open: 1/6–30/8

Situated on north Värmdö by Saxarfjärden, Lillsved offers 49 beds with self-catering. Breakfast also available.

Lyckhem
Skeppsmyra, Björkö
☎ 0176-940 27
Open: Year round, 7/8–20/6 with advance booking

This hostel with adjoining cottages is on Björkö, the peninsula at Arholma northwest of Norrtälje. Go by bus or boat from Stockholm. Stay in rooms with 2–4 beds. Self-catering.

Breakfast and other meals can be ordered. Pub in the pension. Washing machine, sauna. Cycle, canoe and boat rental. Fishing and swimming outings. Sailing and camp schools.

Siarö Fort
Siarö, Ljusterö
☎ 08-542 421 49
Open: 1/5–30/9, May, Sept reservations required

Siarö is a small island near Ljusterö. The hostel houses 30 guests in 2–4 bed rooms. Self-catering and breakfast service. Bathing and fishing. Siarö Fort is a defence installation built on the island in the 1920s. Harbour store. Boat connections to Stockholm.

Stora Kalholmen
South of Finnhamn. For advance bookings, write: c/o Rubin, Storholmsvägen 18, 132 31 Saltsjö-Boo.
☎ 08-542 460 23
Open: 11/6–14/8, otherwise groups only

This hostel is a beautiful villa right by the sea. Space for 22 guests. Go by boat from Stockholm. Stay in rooms with 2–6 beds. Self-catering. Canoe rental. Basic shop. Boats and fishing.

Utö
Gruvbyn, Utö
☎ 08-501 576 60
Open: Year round (closed 16/12–8/1)

This hostel is near Sweden's first iron mine. Takes 44 guests. Go by boat from Västerhaninge, Årsta havsbad (where there is parking) or Stockholm. Stay in rooms with 4 beds, 2 beds during winter. Self-catering. Restaurant, inn and bakery with café in the vicinity. Cycle rental. Guest harbour. Sauna. Shop, post office, boules, tennis courts and mini-golf.

Väddö, Älmsta
Turistgården, Box 9, 760 40 Väddö
☎ 0176-500 78
Open: 28/6–18/8

In Roslagen, by Väddö canal and a few kilometres to the sea, this hostel takes 31 guests. Buses from Stockholm, Norrtälje and Grisslehamn. Stay in rooms with 2–6 beds. Self-catering, meals can be ordered. Running track, cycle rental and football field by the hostel. Swimming, canoe rental, tennis, nine-hole golf course and mini-golf within 3 kilometres. Riding and golf 20 kilometres.

Camping

The Stockholm area offers some 30 camping grounds.
For a complete list including detailed descriptions and maps
you can order our free brochure entitled "Camping Stockholm"
from the Stockholm Information Service ☎ 08-789 24 92.
Listed below is a sampling of these camping areas.

Inner city

Östermalms Citycamping
Fiskartorpsvägen 2, Östermalm
☎ 08-10 29 03
Open: Midsummer to mid-Aug

The site, the most central in Stockholm, is next to Östermalm Idrottsplats (sports ground) near a wooded area for jogging and walking. Within easy reach of the sights and the city centre. One kilometre east of the site is Kampementsbadet with an open-air pool.

Autocamper Stockholm
Långholmen
☎ 070-772 96 60
Open: Midsummer weekend–August

This new camping area on the "green island" right in the heart of Stockholm is specially suited for camper vehicles. Långholmen offers bathing beaches, restaurants and cafés. Toilets, showers, electrical outlets and a pumping station for holding tanks are available on the grounds. No tents or trailers.

Greater Stockholm

Bredäng Camping
Stora Sällskapets väg, Skärholmen
☎ 08-97 70 71
Open: Year round, limited service 1/9–30/4

Beautiful, quiet location, 10 kilometres south of the city centre by Lake Mälaren, 350 metres from Mälarhöjdsbadet (swimming baths). Grassy site with deciduous trees. Sightseeing tours organised. Indoor swimming baths two kilometres, tennis one kilometre, riding one kilometre. Car wash. Dogs allowed.

Eriksöbadets Camping

Eriksövägen 27 B, Vaxholm
☎ 08-541 754 81
Open: 15/4–30/9

Small, child-friendly camping area near Vaxholm, 35 kilometres northeast of Stockholm. Beautiful natural surroundings along Vaxholmsfjärden. Grassy areas are mixed with stands of broadleaf and coniferous trees. Swimming, exercise area and playground.

Flottsbro Camping

Häggstavägen, Huddinge
☎ 08-778 58 60, 778 55 80
Open: Year round, limited service 1/9–31/5

The site is 18 kilometres southwest of the city centre in a natural, undulating setting by Albysjön (Lake Alby). Terraced grassy areas surrounded by mixed woodland. Most plots measure 120–150 square metres. Paths for walks, jogging tracks, "frisbee golf", volleyball etc. Dogs allowed.

Gålö Camping

Skälåker, Haninge
☎ 08-500 331 56
Open: Year round, limited service 1/9–31/5

Camping in the archipelago, with sea bathing, 35 kilometres southeast of the city centre. Rowing boats to hire, fishing. The site is in a quiet, natural, open-air recreation area on a peninsula. Grassy area with deciduous trees. Paths for walks, jogging tracks.

Rösjöbadens Camping

Sollentuna
☎ 08-96 21 84
Open: Year round, limited service 15/9–30/4

Family camp-site beautifully situated by Rösjön open-air pool and recreation area, 15 kilometres north of the city centre. Grassy area surrounded by coniferous woods. Dogs permitted.

Solvalla Citycamping

Sundbergskopplet, Sundyberg
☎ 08-627 03 80
Open: Year round, limited service 1/9–30/4

Camping adjacent to Solvalla horse racing track. Eight kilometres to central Stockholm and two kilometres to Sundyberg Centre. Basic services with toilet and showers in a service module.

Vårbergs Camping

Vårbergsvägen 55, Skärholmen
☎ 08-710 63 70, 710 13 30
Open: 1/6–31/8, limited service over Midsummer weekend

Salmon fishing in central Stockholm with the Foreign Office in the background. Photo: Jeppe Wikström/Pressens Bild

Situated 12 kilometres southwest of Stockholm. Quiet but easily accessed camping spot in the Vårbergs sporting area. Gravel and paved areas with some grassy areas. Tent camping among the oaks. Access to three bathing areas along the Mälaren shore.

Ängby Camping
Blackebergsvägen, Bromma
☎ 08-37 04 20
Open: Year round, limited service 1/10–15/4

Beautifully situated family site 10 kilometres west of the city centre on Lake Mälaren, by Ängby open-air baths. With landing stage, water slide etc. Hilly woodland, mixed coniferous and deciduous trees, grassy and gravelled areas. Tennis, mini-golf, cable TV, boat rentals 1 kilometre. Dogs permitted.

Östnora Camping
Östnora, Västehaninge
☎ 08-500 400 16, off-season 500 295 58
Open: 15/6–31/8

Situated about 40 kilometres south of central Stockholm. Quiet family camping with sea bathing. Grassy areas with mixed coniferous and deciduous trees. Large swimming area with diving platform and pedal-boat rentals. Fine walking trails with excellent mushroom picking.

PRACTICAL INFORMATION

Shops

Normal opening times are 09.30–18.00 weekdays, 09.30–14.00 Saturdays. Many supermarkets are open on Sundays, usually between 12.00 and 16.00. Local shops which sell food and basic goods are often open as late as 23.00. The principal shopping streets in Stockholm are Hamngatan, Biblioteksgatan, Drottninggatan and in the Old Town Västerlånggatan and Österlånggatan, Stora Nygatan and Lilla Nygatan. Suburban centres have many shops with a wide variety of goods.

Emergency

In case of emergency, call ☎ 112 to reach "SOS Alarm" connected to police, ambulance, fire brigade, lifeboats and information on poisoning. For car service and towing call Larmtjänst on ☎ 020-22 00 00 or Assistence-kåren on ☎ 020-91 29 12.

Right of public access

Sweden's unique right of public access (in Swedish, allemans-rätten, lit. "every man's right") means that you can walk freely in the countryside and pick berries, mushrooms and flowers without having to ask permission. But it is forbidden to walk across some-one else's land where plants can be damaged, walk across a garden without permission, tie up boats or swim at private piers and gardens, leave gates open, drop rubbish or make fires in unsuit-able places, break off twigs with-out permission, cut trees, or take grasses, birch-bark, leaves, acorns, nuts, sap, stones, gravel or turf.

Chemists (Pharmacies)

Chemist opening times in the city centre:
C W Scheele, Klarabergsgatan 64 (City) ☎ 08-454 81 30, telefax 08-791 88 77. Open 24 hours, every day.

Mariaapoteket, Torkel Knutssonsgatan 33 (Söder) ☎ 08-669 05 75. Open every day 08.30–22.00.

Vita Björn, Sturegallerian (City Östermalm) ☎ 08-611 09 22. Open Mon–Fri 09.30–22.00; Sat 10.00–17.00; Sun, 12.00–17.00.

Örnen, Odenplan (Vasastan) ☎ 08-736 07 90. Open Mon–Fri 09.00–19.00; weekends 10.00–15.00.

Banks

Normal opening hours for banks are Mon–Fri 09.30–15.00. In the city a number of Handelsbanken's branches are open Mon–Thu until 17.30.

Sparbanken Sverige, Klarabergsgatan 25, opens at 08.30. The main office on Hamngatan is open Mon–Thu 09.30–18.00.

The same opening hours apply for Nordbanken, Hamngatan 12, and SE-Banken at Kungsträdgårdsgatan 8 and Sergels Torg 2.

Car rental

There are several rental agencies in the Stockholm district, renting everything from small cars to trailers. Tourist Centre, Sverige-huset ☎ 08-789 24 90, STF travel bureau ☎ 08-463 22 00 and other tourist offices have more information. The main car rental firms are:

Avis, Sveavägen 61 ☎ 08-34 99 10

Budget, Sveavägen 155 ☎ 08-33 43 83

Europcar Interrent, Hotel Sheraton (City) ☎ 08-21 06 50

Hertz, Vasagatan 26 ☎ 08-24 07 20

Buses

Stockholm's Lokaltrafik, SL, has bus routes both in the town and out to the furthest corners of the district. Buses which run for the most part in the city centre have two-digit numbers: 48, 54 etc. Buses to the suburbs and out-lying towns have three-digit numbers: 202, 307, 430 etc. Adults with children in strollers travel free. As a rule, the bus driver calls out the name of each bus stop. On certain routes there is also a sign in the bus which tells you the name of the next stop. You can, of course, ask the driver if you are unsure. Stockholmskortet (Stockholm card) is valid for all routes (except for airport buses). It's best to show the card to the driver. Maps and timetables are available at the SL information office just inside the main entrance of the Sergels Torg subway station, or at most Pressbyrå kiosks.

Tipping

Tipping is not as self-evident in Sweden as in many other countries. Hotel and taxi bills all have the tip included. If you want to you can add on 10 per cent as a tip. This is common practice at restaurants where you feel the service has been good. At cloakrooms there is usually some indication as to how much the cloakroom attendant takes, between 10 and 20 kronor.

Baggage lockers

Baggage lockers can be found at Centralstationen, in most large stores and at a number of underground stations. There are also boxes at Tegelvikshamn, Värtahamnen and the Viking Lines terminal. A word of warning about the boxes at Centralstationen: There are a number of false keys in circulation. Baggage can be left for safe-keeping on the lower level of Centralstationen ☎ 08-762 25 50.

Guides

There is an association of well-educated, polyglot tourist guides, authorised by the Stockholm Information Service. Guide and Group Tours, located in the Tourist Centre in Sverigehuset delegates guides, group tours and buses on order ☎ 08-789 24 96. Book well in advance.

Lost property

Centralstationen, lower ground floor ☎ 08-762 25 50

Police's lost property office, Bergsgatan 39 ☎ 08-401 07 88

SL lost property office, Rådmansgatan T-bana station ☎ 08-736 07 80

Waxholmsbolaget, Nybrokajen 2 ☎ 08-692 18 20

Railway information

Centralstationen, domestic ☎ 020-75 75 75, international ☎ 020-75 75 75, 08-696 75 40 Östra station, local trains northwards ☎ 08-600 10 00

Religious services

There are approximately 160 churches in the Stockholm area, including places of worship representing a number of religions and denominations.

Catholic Churches:
Domkyrkan, Folkungagatan 46
☎ 08-640 00 81;

Santa Eugenia Church, Kungsträdgårdsgatan 12
☎ 08-679 57 70

Synagogues:
The Great Synagogue, Wahrendorffsgatan 3A
☎ 08-679 29 00 (Conservative);

Adas Jisroel, St Paulsgatan 13
☎ 08-644 19 95 (Orthodox);

Adas Jeschurun, Riddargatan 5
☎ 08-611 91 61 (Orthodox)

Protestant services in English:
St Peter & St Sigfrid, Anglican/
Episcopal Church, Strandvägen
76 ☎ 08-663 82 48

Santa Clara Church, United Christian Congregation, Klarabergsgatan ☎ 08-723 30 29

Immanuel Church, International Fellowship, Kungstensgatan 17
☎ 08-674 13 00

For more information, call Stiftskansliet ☎ 08-781 01 00.

Local commuter trains

In addition to the underground and buses, Stockholm's Lokaltrafik, SL, operates commuter trains covering a wider area than the underground. From the Central Station you can get to Kungsängen and Märsta in the northwest and to Nynäshamn and Gnesta in the southwest and southeast respectively. It takes nine minutes to get to the Stockholm trade fair (Stockholmsmässan) at Älvsjö. Other types of commuter trains are the historic Roslagsbanan and the more modern Saltsjöbanan. Roslagsbanan leaves from Östra Station at SUBWAY Tekniska Högskolan and goes north to Kårsta and Åkersberga. Saltsjöbanan goes from SUBWAY Slussen out to Saltsjöbaden in the east. Nockebybanan (tram) and Lidingöbanan run in the southern parts of Bromma and Lidingö, respectively. See Commuter train map, page 152.

Health care

In case of emergency, ring:
☎ 112 and ask for an ambulance. In case of severe poisoning call Giftinformationscentralen

(Poison Information Centre) ☎ 112. In less acute cases, ring ☎ 08-33 12 31. Any hospital will take you in in the event of physical injury. For emergency psychiatric care, contact the local hospital nearest your temporary address. If you have doubts or queries, call health care information at ☎ 08-644 92 00. Free health care advice is also given at this number. A private alternative is Cityakuten, Holländargatan 3 ☎ 08-411 71 77.

Dentist

Emergency surgery, Flemingatan 22 (St Eriks Sjukhus on Kungsholmen) ☎ 08-654 11 17. Open every day 08.00–20.00. No bookings. After 19.00, only emergency cases such as accidents, bleeding etc. are taken in. After 21.00, call ☎ 08-644 92 00 for more information.

Police

In case of emergency, call ☎ 112. Do you want to ask or inform the police about something? Then contact the nearest Police Station. Listed below are some of the Police Stations in central Stockholm:

City Precinct, Flemmingatan 14 ☎ 08-401 10 00; Brunkebergstorg 1–3; Central Station ☎ 08-401 12 76; Tulegatan 4 ☎ 08-401 13 60, 401 14 50; Norrtullsgatan 4 ☎ 08-401 12 00; St. Eriksgatan 44, 1st floor ☎ 08-401 11 51.

Local Police Stations in Södermalm are located at the following addresses: Hornsbruksgatan 28, 3rd floor ☎ 08-401 15 01; Tjärhovsgatan 21 ☎ 08-401 02 78; Fatbursgatan 1, 2nd floor ☎ 08-401 15 51.

South of the city: Farstaplan 2, Farsta ☎ 08-401 20 00. Jakobsdalsvägen 1, Nacka Strand ☎ 08-401 60 00. Björnkullavägen 9, Huddinge ☎ 08-401 70 00. Jovisgatan 5, Södertälje ☎ 08-401 80 00.

West of the city: Solnavägen 98, Solna ☎ 08-401 30 00.

North of the city: Biblioteksgången 11, Täby ☎ 08-401 40 00. Tingsvägen 27, Sollentuna ☎ 08-401 50 00. Arlanda Airport ☎ 08-797 90 00.

The Central Police Station (Polishuset) is on Kungsholmen at Agnegatan 33–37 ☎ 08-401 00 00. The same

Take the bus to Vaxholm and visit Vaxholm Castle with its museum describing the history of the fortress. Photo: Claes Löfgren/Pressens Bild

number can be used for questions or information.

Post

The post office headquarters is on Vasagatan 28–34, near Centralstationen ☎ 08-781 20 40. Open Mon–Fri 09.00–18.00, Sat 10.00–13.00. Poste Restante is available. The Central Station's post office ☎ 08-781 20 41 is open Mon–Fri 07.00–22.00, weekends 10.00–19.00. Other post offices in Stockholm and the district are listed in the "Företag A–Ö" telephone directory.

Radio programmes

Radio Stockholm broadcasts on FM 103.3. Stockholm International broadcasts in English and several other languages on FM 89.6.

Sightseeing

Stockholm has a great variety of sightseeing tours by both bus and boat. Tickets and information for all city tours are available at the Excursion Shop in Sweden House on Hamngatan.

Bus tours: City Sightseeing, Gustav Adolfs Torg in front of the Opera House ☎ 08-411 70 23.

Stockholm Sightseeing,
Stadshusbron, Strömkajen,
Nybroplan ☎ 08-24 04 70.

Stockholmskortet (Stockholm card)

The Stockholm Card costs 175
kronor for 24 hours (1996) and is
valid for one adult and two children under 18. Included are the
following: Free trips by bus (apart
from airport buses), underground, local trains. Free parking
at all meters and council-owned
parking places in Stockholm city
district. Free boat sightseeing
with Stockholm Sightseeing's
chosen tours. Free bus sightseeing with City Sight's chosen
tours. Boat to Drottningholm,
return trip for the price of a
single. Exhibition offer, two for
the price of one. Free entry to 70
museums and or sights. Ten per
cent refund on tickets to performances at the Concert House and
10 per cent refund on Skansen's
glassworks assortment.

Tax-free

Citizens of non-Nordic/Scandi-
navian countries can buy goods
free of VAT/sales tax in all the
larger shops. Certain rules apply.

You can get a special folder about
tax-free shopping at the tourist
bureau.

Taxis

There are many taxi companies
in Stockholm, and prices can
vary. A taxi hailed in the street
may in certain cases charge a
much higher rate than a taxi
associated with one of the larger
companies. The largest of these is
Taxi Stockholm ☎ 08-15 00 00.
Other companies are Taxi Kurir
☎ 08-30 00 00 and Taxi 020 ☎
020-93 93 93. Taxis to and from
Arlanda should not cost more
than 350 kronor (1996). SAS has
a limousine service to and from
Arlanda and allows several
people to share one car. Prices to
and from the city are a little
cheaper than taking a single taxi
☎ 08-797 37 00.
Note: always check the price
before your ride begins.

Taxi guides

Ride in a taxi with a trained
sightseeing guide as your driver.
Prices are about 400 kronor per
hour. Also ask about touring trips
outside the city. Prices should be
lower. Booking ☎ 08-789 24 96.

Newspapers

You can read foreign newspapers at Stadsbiblioteket (the city library), Sveavägen 73 and at Kulturhuset, Sergels Torg. If you want to buy your own newspaper, try the Centralstationen or some of the subway station kiosks.

Toilets

Gallerian. Sergels Torg, T-Centralen. Hötorget, T-bana. Östermalmstorg, T-bana. Birger Jarlsgatan, T-bana. Rotundan, Norra Bantorget. Slottet, Västra Valvet. Skeppsbron. Slussen, Gula gången. Skanstull, Ringen.

Fridhemsplan, Fridhemsgatan. Odenplan. Strandvägen, Djurgårdsbron. Vasaparken, summer Jun–Aug. Kungsträdgården, Jun–Aug.

Tunnelbana (T-bana; underground/subway/metro)

With its 110 kilometres of rails and 100 stations, Stockholm's underground system is one of the largest in the world. Furthermore, the stretch from Kungsträdgården to Akalla/ Hjulsta is the world's longest art exhibition. Each station has been decorated by artists, and the result makes the

Art in the Stockholm underground. Each station on the line from Kungsträdgården to Akalla/Hjulsta has been designed by artists. The mural shown above is from T-centralen. Photo: Stockholm Information Service

trip well worth your while. Kungsträdgården, T-Centralen, Rådhuset, Fridhemsplan and Solna Centrum stations have won international recognition. SL's tourist card and coupons are sold in the kiosks of Pressbyrån and at Centralstationen. They are valid for T-bana, bus and commuter trains. See the map of the T-bana network on page 152.

Turistkort (tourist card)

SL sells tourist cards for an unlimited number of journeys by bus, T-bana and local trains. Tourist cards for 24 hours cost 56 kronor (1996). Tourist cards for 72 hours cost 107 kronor and are also valid for entry to Skansen, Kaknästornet and Gröna Lund. Cards cost 33 kronor for pensioners and 70 kronor for people under 18 years of age. The card is also valid for trams and ferries to Djurgården and for entry to the Tramway Museum (Spårvagnsmuseet). See also Stockholmskort.

Tourist bureaux

Stockholm: The Tourist Centre, Stockholm's largest tourist bureau, is in Sweden House (opposite NK department store) ☎ 08-789 24 90. You'll find maps, books and answers to most of your questions. The Sweden Bookshop has literature about Sweden published in a variety of languages.

The Excursion Shop, in the same office, sells tours and organised excursions ☎ 08-789 24 15.

The third year-round tourist bureau in Stockholm is in Kaknäs Tower ☎ 08-789 24 35.

From the beginning of May until the end of October, there is an office in City Hall ☎ 08-651 21 12.

The Hotel Central, in Central Station, will help you find a hotel room ☎ 08-24 08 80.

For tourists driving cars up from the south, there is a summertime tourist office in Kungens Kurva, Skärholmen ☎ 08-710 13 20.

For telephone numbers to tourist offices throughout the greater Stockholm area, call the Tourist Centre ☎ 08-789 24 90.

MAPS

Stockholm region. On the next pages Central Stockholm

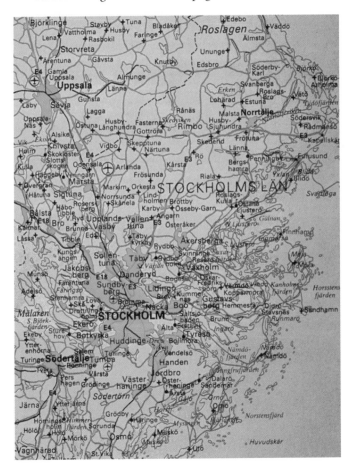

Spårtrafik

Stockholm • Rail network

SL Trafikupplysning / Information
08-600 10 00

T Tunnelbanan
Hässelby-Farsta/Hagsätra/Skarpnäck
Ropsten/Mörby centrum-Fruängen/Norsborg
Akalla/Hjulsta-Kungsträdgården

J Pendeltågen
Märsta-Södertälje-Gnesta
Kungsängen-Västerhaninge-Nynäshamn

Nockebybanan
Alvik-Nockeby

Lidingöbanan
Ropsten-Lidingö

J Roslagsbanan
Stockholm Ö-Näsbypark/Österskär/Kårsta

J Saltsjöbanan
Slussen-Saltsjöbaden/Solsidan

⊙ Bytesstation/Interchange station

Grafisk form: G. Månsson

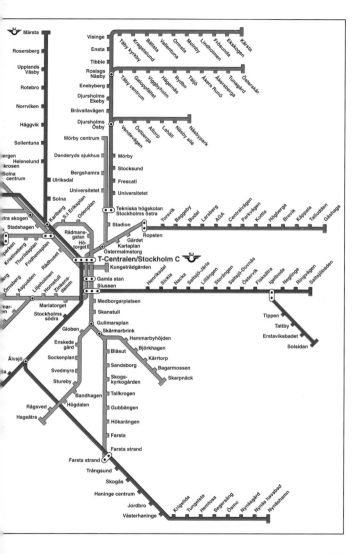

INDEX

Twilight over the Stockholm Globe. Photo: Malcolm Hanes/Pressens Bild

STOCKHOLM
BEAUTY ON WATER

Loads to see and do in Stockholm!

Stockholm's five official tourist offices can help you with tourist information, suggestions about what is going on in the city, ticket purchase and everything else you need to know for a fun stay in Stockholm. Tourist offices are located at the following places in the city:

Sweden House, Hamngatan 27
Tourist Centre +46 8-789 24 90,
fax +46 8-789 24 91, E-mail info@stoinfo.se
Tourist information, sales of local transport cards, tourist passes, maps and guide books.
Utflyktsbutiken +46 8-789 24 15,
fax +46 8-789 24 91 Excursion packages, ticket sales (Note! No telephone bookings), cabin rental and direct hotel bookings.
Guide- and group bookings +46 8-789 24 96,
fax +46 8-789 24 45 Booking of authorised guides, buses and group arrangements.
Sweden Shop +46 8-789 24 06 Souvenirs and Swedish handicrafts.
Sweden Book Shop +46 8-789 21 31 Swedish literature translated to other languages.
Forex +46 8-20 03 89 Foreign exchange.

Hotellcentralen, Central Station
+46 8-24 08 80, fax +46 8-791 86 66,
E-mail hotels@stoinfo.se
Pre-booking and direct booking of hotel rooms, tourist information and sales of tourist passes, maps and guidebooks.

Kaknäs Tower, Gärdet
+46 8-789 24 35, fax +46 8-667 85 07,
E-mail kaknas@stoinfo.se
Tourist information, souvenirs and the highest view-point in Scandinavia with a café and restaurant.

City Hall, Hantverkargatan 1
Tourist information and souvenirs. Open during summer months and on weekends during the winter.

Info Stop Stockholm, Kungens Kurva, exit E4 south of Stockholm
Tourist information, direct booking of hotels and youth hostels. Open during the summer months.

Stockholm This Week
If you want to find out more about what is going on in Stockholm you should look for the tourist guide, Stockholm This Week. Published once a month, it is available from tourist offices, most hotels and certain restaurants around Stockholm.

The Stockholm Card
The Stockholm Card gives you free entrance to more than 70 museums and attractions and can be bought at all the tourist offices in Stockholm.

Information kiosks – Stockholm Today
Information Kiosks have been set up at 14 places around Stockholm comprising a touch-screen controlled computer, a printer and a telephone. This allows the visitor to Stockholm to find information about various activities, sights and events described in words, images and in video sequences. Information is available in Swedish, English, German and French. All pages are printable and, by using the telephone it is possible to dial up more information or make hotel bookings free of charge.

Internet
Stockholm's official pages about up-to-the-minute tourist information, hints about what to do and see, a hotel guide and lots more are now available on the Internet on: http://www.stoinfo.se

STOCKHOLM INFORMATION SERVICE
CONVENTION & VISITORS BUREAU

of the king's creations, and its 18 members, commonly known as "the eighteen", meet on the top floor of the stock exchange building.

Once a week "the eighteen" go to another part of Gamla Stan. The restaurant Den Gyldene Freden is to be found on Järntorget, and there, in the Bellman rooms, the traditional Thursday suppers are held. The restaurant has been a meeting place for Stockholm poets since the 18th century – first Bellman, then Stagnelius and more recently Nils Ferlin and Evert Taube. The artist Anders Zorn bought the building in 1919 for 150,000 kronor and later bequeathed it in his will to the Swedish Academy.

Changing of the guard at the Royal Palace. Photo: Hans Nelsäter/Bildarkivet

Martial Music

The parade that marches to the Royal Palace for the changing of the guard each day is one of Stockholm's most popular tourist attractions. Best of all is when the Lifeguard Dragoons ride by on horseback in their fine uniforms and polished spiked helmets, playing music. The changing of the guard takes place on weekdays at 12.15 between June and August and on Wednesdays and Saturdays at the same time during the remainder of the year. On Sundays it is held at 13.15 (all year round).

The Village Church That Grew

Storkyrkan (main, or big, church) is Stockholm's cathedral and the city's oldest church. There, prior to 1279, the "Village Church" was first mentioned in a document. Only a few bricks in the outside wall remain to remind us of its 13th-century existence. Take a look at the high rib vaulting (from the 15th century), gilded royal boxes and pulpit of the beautiful interior. A fine mediaeval sculpture here depicts St George and the dragon. The saint symbolises Sweden, and the fire-breathing dragon is the enemy, Denmark. King Sten Sture the Elder ordered the statue in memory of the victory over the Danes at Brunkebergsåsen in 1471.

Storkyrkan is Stockholm's principal cathedral. Photo: Jan Collsiöö/ Pressens Bild

---

Another well-known Swedish artist, Carl Larsson, was born near Järntorget. A plaque on the house at Prästgatan (Priest Street) 78 reminds us of his early days there. You can get there by way of the narrowest street in Gamla Stan, Mårten Trotzigs gränd, in some places no more than 90 centimetres wide.

Prästgatan is easy to miss the first time you visit Gamla Stan. It runs parallel to the much more frequented Västerlånggatan, which has a wider variety of shops. However, Prästgatan contains more of the Old Town's genuine history.

Surprisingly enough, it is the only street in Gamla Stan (and consequently in Stockholm) which can be said to be truly mediaeval. Its name is derived, of course, from those who lived there during the 16th century.

Yet the small part of Prästgatan to the north of Storkyrkobrinken (Church Hill) used to be known as Helwitesgatun (Hell Street). It's said the hangman's house used to be there.

Vikings and Princes

We are reminded of the Viking period by a runestone in the walls of one of the houses on the corner of Kåkbrinken (House Hill) and Prästgatan. The inscription reads, "Torsten and Frögun had this stone set up here in memory of their son".

The period most represented in Gamla Stan is the Great Power era of the 17th century. Most of the houses date from that epoch.

On the neighbouring island Riddarholmen (Knight's island) are the large private palaces built by the great generals of that time: Wrangel Palace, which now houses the Svea Hovrätt (Swedish civil and criminal appellate court), Stenbockska Palace, which contains the supreme admin-

A bit of cheery music and entertainment livens up tired wanderers on Österlånggatan in Gamla Stan. Photo: Hans Nelsäter/Bildarkivet

Riddarholmen's three, large private palaces: Wrangelska Palace, Stenbockska Palace and Bondeska Palace. Photo: Hans Nelsäter/Bildarkivet

istrative court, and Bondeska Palace, where the Supreme Court has its offices.

Gamla Stan also contains some former private palaces: Axel Oxenstierna's palace is at Storkyrkobrinken 2 and now houses the department of education. Directly opposite the Royal Palace on Slottsbacken is Tessinska Palace, where the palace designer Nicodemus Tessin the Younger once lived. The Stockholm County governor (equivalent of a lord lieutenant) now lives there.

The houses along busy Skeppsbron are otherwise the most obvious example of 17th-century Great Power pomp. They were built by rich merchants, the Skeppsbro nobility, to show Europe that the Swedish capital was something to be reckoned with.

And from Skeppsbron it isn't far to Söder.

The South Side

There's something special about Söder (the South Side).
Once solidly working class, now mildly upscale, the district
radiates a feeling of human warmth and openness
right in the middle of the city.

Söder isn't quite as much of a rat race as the other parts of town. Söder folk take life as it comes. At the same time, they are very proud of their part of town.

On the top of the hill at Hornsgatan, directly opposite Maria Magdalena church (where Evert Taube is buried), art lovers can find small but well-reputed galleries. For example, the craft group Blås och Knåda (Blow and Knead) has its boutique there, as does the glasswork artist Erik Höglund.

Söder and boats along Söder Mälarstrand. Photo: Jeppe Wikström/Pressens Bild

Pleasant Blend

Another sloping street is that at the beginning of dead-straight Götgatan with its heavy traffic. Here, pub lovers can pick and choose, for the area boasts more pubs than any other in Stockholm.

Yet even there you'll find a motley assortment of small businesses: a second-hand book shop, a music shop, a furniture shop specialising in Swedish design and Carl Malmsten furniture, an undertaker, an antique shop and a boutique with Tiogruppens ("Group of Ten") colourful fabrics and handicrafts – to name but a few.

Söder's third largest street from Södermalmstorg is Katarinavägen. It, too, is straight, but it doesn't have any shops. Constructed shortly after the turn of the century, it was at first thought to be too big. Now it is a light and airy place in which to walk, as well as being the main road it was intended to be, and runs to the western part of Söder with Fjällgatan as the main tourist attraction.

"The Fluttering Corn-Cob"

No winger has ever played football quite like Lennart "Nacka" Skoglund. He was the idol, the dribbler, the lad from Söder in the striped Hammarby F C shirt. As well as playing astounding football with the Italian Inter club, Nacka led a life of luxury. He was known in Italy as the "fluttering corn-cob" because of the colour of his hair and the way he moved. But back in Sweden he wasn't able to live up to the myths that had grown around him. He broke down and played his last matches on a team made up of fellow alcoholics. He died, aged 45, on 8 July 1975.

*The great striker "Nacka" Skoglund.
Photo: Jonny Graan/Pressens Bild*

Fjällgatan offers one of the best views over Stockholm. Photo: Bengt Hedberg/ Naturbild

Cultural History on Fjällgatan

The artists who have painted Söder's genuine 18th-century street are innumerable, as are the tourists who go there each summer to enjoy the view. Not much is left of the original Fjällgatan (Hill Street). The fact that it remains at all is due in great part to Anna Lindhagen, who wrote a book in 1923 and started a movement to save the city's old buildings, in particular those on Fjällgatan where she lived. In the 1600s it was known as Galgbergsgatan (Gallow Hill Street) after the local execution site.

There is no typical Söder architectural style. The low wooden houses painted red and known as Söderkåkar were originally built by and for working-class people. These are now listed buildings of rare cultural value, and examples can be seen at Åsöberget in the western part of Söder. Elsewhere in Söder you will see giant blocks from the 1960s built

On the heights of Söder houses are hidden behind greenery and red gates. Photo: Hans Nelsäter/Bildarkivet

alongside beautiful 18th-century houses, and fin-de-siècle Jugendstil mixed in with modern creations.

The newest and most talked about buildings are in the Södra station area. Someone has likened it to "walking into an architectural competition". The area is Sweden's most densely inhabited, with about 8000 people living in an area the size of 40 football fields. The most well known of these buildings is the Bow, a semicircular building located at Medborgarplatsen (Citizens' Square), designed by the Spanish architect Ricardo Bofill. A recent addition to the area is a controversial "skyscraper".

Something else you can visit at Medborgarplatsen is Söderhallarna (Söder Halls), one of Stockholm's three market halls complete with boutiques, cafés, restaurants and delicatessens.

Small and Large

Buildings of quite another nature can be found in Eriksdalslund and Tantolunden. There you'll find the small colonies (workers' cottages) and their flower garden plots squeezed up against one another, making quite a contrast to life in the city. Some families live far out in the suburbs

The parks of Eriksdalslunden and Tantolunden are home to tightly placed garden cottages such as these. Photo: Bror Hjälmrud/Bildhuset

Boat ride through the still waters of the Långholmen Canal. Photo: Hans Nelsäter/Bildarkivet

of Stockholm, only to move in to a cottage and the town in spring to live "in the country". The plots at Eriksdalslund are amongst the oldest in Stockholm and were first cultivated in 1906.

One of Stockholm's smallest parks is Ivar Lo's Park by Bastugatan. It is named after the author Ivar Lo-Johansson, and its sandboxes and slide are a particular favourite of children. Parents can enjoy the superb view across Riddarfjärden.

Långholmen (Long Island) is a much bigger park. In fact, it is an open-air space with several buildings of cultural and historical interest. Långholmen was the city's prison island for 250 years, an era that came to an end in 1975 when the beaches were opened for walks. The old local prison is now a hotel and youth hostel.

The traffic moves across Västerbron (West Bridge) on Långholmen, in one direction to Hornstull on Söder, in the other to Kungsholmen.

The King's Island

The flats on Kungsholmen (King's island) are, as in all the inner parts of the city, extremely attractive, and include some of the most expensive dwellings per square metre in the country. But that wasn't so when the Fire Mill burned down...

"When the Fire Mill burned down" is an old saying that refers to the tremendous fire which illuminated the Stockholm skyline on the last night of October 1878. The disaster occurred at a steam mill which had revolutionised the Swedish flour industry in the early 19th century. The mill (Eldkvarn) was located on the site of the present-day City Hall.

At that time, Kungsholmen was a poor part of the city where badly paid workers sweated out their lives in tedious industrial jobs. The best known of these factories was Bolinders, which made machine parts for industry and the railroads as well as for stoves, ovens, fountains, sofas and ornaments made of cast iron, a fashionable material at that time.

One of the 19th century's greatest inventions, Gustaf de Laval's milk separator, was made on Kungsholmen at Separator's factory. The machine achieved universal renown as the first that could separate milk from cream in a continuous flow.

Quiet Islet

A change of name brought little change in fortune. Still, Kungsholmen has changed names a number of times. At first it was called Liderne, which comes from the Old Swedish word for slope or hillside. Then it became Munklägret (Monks' Camp), after the Franciscan monks who owned the island before Gustav Vasa incorporated it into the Crown at the time of the Reformation.

The island received its present name towards the end of the 1600s. At that time Karl XI was king, Sweden was a great power and Stockholm was

Three gilded crowns over Kungsholmen. Photo: Jeppe Wikström/Pressens Bild

truly recognised as the capital. This time it was the king's turn to be honoured. After all, the knights and the queen had their islands, respectively Riddarholm and Drottningholm.

Today, Kungsholmen is something of a small town within the city. Stockholmers say "it's quiet on Kungsholmen". What they mean is that entertainment and commercial life are not as noticeable here as in other parts of town. For example, there are no cinemas left on Kungsholmen but there are many new local pubs well worth visiting.

Having said that, things are not always quiet on Kungsholmen. Many of the country's criminals have been resident there, in Kronoberg prison to be precise. The prison functions as a sort of stopover place whilst criminals are waiting to be tried and, in the case of a conviction, to be moved to one of the country's criminal institutions. No one has yet succeeded in escaping from the newly built part of the prison.

There is an underground tunnel, the "Sigher's Walk", which leads to Rådhuset (the court house) where judgement is passed. But it isn't simply decisive judgements such as "guilty" or "not guilty" that are passed in the Rådhuset. A twice-uttered "yes" means that the couple who have had a civil wedding will hopefully live happily ever after.

Built in 1909–15 after designs by Carl Westman, the Rådhuset has one of the most decorated interiors of any building in the city, with paintings and sculptures by, amongst others, Olle Hjortzberg, Christian Eriksson and the brothers Aron and Gustaf Sandberg. Outside, it is reminiscent of Vadstena Castle in its Vasa-inspired renaissance style.

The City Hall is the building on Kungsholmen with the most character, but you can also see the two large newspaper publishing offices especially well from Västerbron. Dagens Nyheter/Expressen is the tallest, with 24 floors. Svenska Dagbladet contents itself with 14.

Stockholm's patron saint, Eric, the King of Sweden during the 12th

Stockholmers enjoying the sandy beach at Smedsuddsbadet on Kungsholmen.
Photo: Hans Nelsäter/Bildarkivet

century, has a street named after him. It is called St Eriksgatan (St Eric's Street) and runs from Kungsholmen across St Eriksbron (St Eric's Bridge) far into Vasastan.

The Västerbron connects Kungsholmen to Södermalm and is one of the city's best-known silhouettes. Photo: Mark Markefelt/Pressens Bild

The Bridge in the West

Bridges are important for "the city on the water". Västerbron is the largest, at 610 metres long and 29 metres high. It is Sweden's largest arched bridge. All the same, it is nothing to boast about – there are lots of larger and longer bridges.

But the spare style of the spans is beautiful. The bridge was completed in 1935. These days, bungy jumpers sometimes do their thing from Västerbron. Another bit of derring-do is to fly a small plane between the bridge spans.

Vasastan

Vasastan is the large part of Stockholm
to the north of the city. Construction began in earnest
as late as the 1880s, by which time wood was definitely
out of date in Stockholm. Vasastan's stone buildings
and its distance from the water have given rise
to the name "the Stone Desert".

Vasastan was long regarded as a suburb of Stockholm. Or more accurately, since it was only partly constructed, a collection of several suburbs. The foremost example is "Siberia", which lies between Odengatan and Vanadislunden and was, at the turn of the century, the most densely populated part of the town. At that time it was surrounded by meadows,

Lush parks and gardens surround many houses in Vasastan. Photo: Hans Nelsäter/Bildarkivet

Bargains are waiting to be found in the antique and second-hand shops on Odengatan. Photo: Folke Hellberg/Pressens Bild

cattle and barns. Now the borders to the rest of Vasastan's built-up area have been erased.

Around Odenplan, in the heart of Vasastan, are any number of small and large shops and local restaurants, and several theatres. The central church is called Gustav Vasa's church. It is in the new baroque style, designed by Agi Lindegren, and was consecrated in 1906.

A popular shopping street is that part of Odengatan directly opposite Vasaparken. There are small antique shops that cater both to the well-heeled and to curiosity seekers, as well as a shop where you can buy stylish men's clothes and another for second-hand clothes. Roslagsgatan is another street that is frequented by antique hunters.

A special calm lies over nearby Vasaparken, despite the fact that American football training as well as Japanese shadow boxing take place there during the summer. The park is a popular place for the people of Vasastan to sunbathe and play boules. In winter, the playing areas are cleared and hosed for ice-skating.

A Historic District

At St Eriksplan, in the part of Vasastan known as Birkastan, is the beginning of one of Stockholm's most charming streets, Rörstrandsgatan, which features a variety of small shops and restaurants.

During the Middle Ages there was a village here called Rörstrand, but the area is known above all as the place where Rörstrands Porcelain factory manufactured porcelain and faience. The Stockholm epoch lasted for 200 years, from 1726 to 1926, when the factory was pulled down and manufacturing moved to Gothenburg.

Norra Bantorget (North Railway Square) nudges right up to the city. It belongs to the part of town which is really Norrmalm, a name seldom used nowadays. These days, Norra Bantorget is regarded as being on the boundary between Vasastan and the city. Before the railways were built out and the Central Station was inaugurated in 1871, the square sat beside a railway station.

Today, Norra Bantorget is known as the headquarters for Sweden's Labour Movement. The "LO-borgen" (trade union fort) and Folkets hus (the people's house) are there. In the early days of Norra Bantorget, in the 17th century, an orphanage for the poor children of the town occupied the site where Folkets hus is today. The district is consequently known as Barnhuset (orphanage). There was also a place called Rosenkammaren (the rose chamber), but the name belies its history: Rosenkammaren used to be a torture chamber. There is a street running from Norra Bantorget which was called Tunnelgatan (Tunnel Street) for a hundred years, until 1 May 1986. Its name was then changed to Olof Palmes Gata, in memory of the prime minister who was assassinated on 28 February 1986 on the corner of Sveavägen and Tunnelgatan.

Clear Silhouette

Sveavägen is the broad, tree-lined but busy road which runs from Sergels Torg in the central city to the edge of Vasastan.

It ends at the Wenner-Gren Centre. This is an international research centre which was in part financed by the great financier Axel Wenner-

Norra Bantorget in the early 1870s in a panorama by Heinrich Neuhaus.
Photo: Francis Bruun/Stockholms Stadsmuseum

Gren. Amongst other things, he founded Electrolux in 1919 and maintained ownership until 1956. But he was unlucky with other enterprises such as the monorail Alweg, and in companies in the Bahamas and in Mexico. The tall building "Wenner-Gren-Scraper" is, however, a building which has improved with the passing of time. It was designed by Sune Lindström and Alf Bydén and built in 1960.

Observatorielunden (Observatory Meadow) is a park which can easily be missed. It still retains some of its academic character, even if the majority of the university buildings have been at Frescati, northeast of the city, since the 1960s. Handelshögskolan (the prestigious business school), the "old" Stockholm University encircle Observatorielunden.

Interior from the Strindberg Museum on Drottninggatan 85. Photo: Anders Rising/Tiofoto

Strindberg's Stockholm

August Strindberg moved house a number of times in Stockholm – 25, all told – living the first and last years of his life in Vasastan. He lived at Norrtullsgatan 14 (North Toll Street) on three different occasions when he was young and knew the property, a farm with grazing cows, apple trees and a greenhouse. It was at Norrtulls-gatan 14 that Strindberg met Siri von Essen, the unhappy wife of a guards officer. Between 1907 and 1912 Strindberg lived in Blå Tornet, the "Blue Tower" at Drottninggatan 85. The flat in Blå Tornet is the only place where Strindberg lived in Stockholm and abroad which has been preserved for posterity in its original style.

The City Library attracts readers of all ages. Photo: Lennart Rooth/Pressens Bild

The City Library – A Functional Book Box

Basically a cube with a cylinder on top, Stadsbiblioteket (the City Library) is one of Stockholm's most famous and, many think, most beautiful buildings. It has elements of 1920s classicism, but above all it can be seen as a predecessor of "functional" architecture. Light and air, simplicity and consistency play important parts in the character of the building, designed by Gunnar Asplund, the greatest of the Swedish functionalists. Asplund was the chief architect at the Stockholm Exhibition in 1930 when functionalism was first introduced to Sweden.

The walk up to Observatorielunden is worth the trouble. There you'll find Carl Hårleman's observatory of 1735. The house and its tower were used until the beginning of the 1930s for astronomic research. Nowadays it is a museum.

From over the fence up on the hill it's easy to look down across the roofs of Vasastan, the city and Östermalm.

Östermalm

Cut-glass chandeliers and mink coats:
there are a lot of them in Östermalm. Just as there are
exclusive antique and furniture shops. This eastern side
of town is, in a manner of speaking, established.

But hear and wonder all ye citizens! Social Democracy has close connections with Östermalm. The whole of Karlavägen was full of red ban-
ners when tens of thousands of 1st of May demonstrators marched off to
Gärdet (the Meadow) at the turn of the century. Twenty years earlier,
socialist pioneers like August Palm and Hjalmar Branting had made
their way to Östermalm to hold meetings.

At that time Östermalm was undergoing a great change. It was to be
posh. So posh that the old name Ladugårdslandet ("barn plot", known
colloquially as Laggårslanne) wouldn't be allowed to remain. Old shacks
were pulled down to be replaced by elegant flats. Dynamite manufactured by Nobel was used to blast away "all these repugnancies which un-
dermine the health of the body, together with these dirty and dull souls,"
as the town planner Albert Lindhagen described Östermalm and its residents.

The Royal District

Humlegårdsgatan (Hop-yard Street) runs from Östermalmstorg down
to Humlegården. Hops are, of course, one of the ingredients of beer. The
Royal Court cultivated hops in the park during the 17th century.

Kungliga Biblioteket (the Royal Library) is not the only building in
Humlegården; there are two or three others, but the library is the most
distinctive. If you're in a literary frame of mind and want to see a fine
room, you should visit the reading room. Many Swedish writers and re-
searchers have engrossed themselves in the books at KB, Sweden's national library. It's not a lending library, but you can of course ask for

Parade carriage à la Daumont, outside court stables. Photo: Gösta Kylsberg

books to read there. There's a great deal to choose from – essentially all the books printed in Sweden since 1661, as well as a good selection in English.

Another remarkable "royal object" in Östermalm is Hovstallet (the court stables). It is large, the same size as a whole block of houses. Hovstallet is at Dramaten; the entrance is at Väpnargatan, and the interior is surprisingly beautiful. There are horses (which are out to pasture in summer), coaches and carriages used for royal processions, among which you will find the state coach. Guided tours are conducted on Saturdays and Sundays at 14.00.

Strandvägen (Shore Road) is the most ostentatious street on Östermalm, and indeed in the whole of Stockholm. In reality it is neither a street nor a road. It is an esplanade, with trees planted between the traffic lanes.

The houses, or palaces as they were to be called, were built for wealthy wholesalers, company directors and forest barons in the newly rich in-

Following pages: Strandvägen early in the morning before the city has come to life. Photo: Lennart Hyse/Pressens Bild

dustrialised Sweden which came into being at the end of the 19th century.

At the beginning of Strandvägen, that is at Nybroviken, is the interior decorator shop Svenskt Tenn (Swedish Tin).

The museum trams which run from Norrmalmstorg along Strandvägen to Djurgården provide a picturesque addition to this part of town. While it is said to have been expensive to lay down the tracks and build tram sheds, it now seems worth it. Simply climb aboard for a nostalgic trip.

Immediately after Djurgårdsbron (Djurgård's Bridge), Strandvägen

Fresh greens and other delicacies are available in Östermalmshallen. Photo: Hans Nelsäter/Bildarkivet

Östermalm Hall

Östermalm Hall is a meeting place for gourmets. About 20 sellers offer all sorts of delicacies, and there are several excellent cafés and lunch restaurants between the stands. The Hall, as locals call it, is at Östermalmstorg and is, despite the prices, a joy to experience. You can always browse for free.

Bergman Territory

The director Ingmar Bergman has many connections with Östermalm. He grew up first on Valhallavägen and then in a parish house at Östermalmstorg. His father was the minister at Hedvig Eleonora church. His childhood cinema was Fågel Blå (Bluebird) at Skeppargatan 60. He has directed many films at the Film House studios near Gärdet, including Fanny and Alexander. From 1963–66 he was the director of Dramaten (the Royal Theatre), where he still occasionally directs.

Director Ingmar Bergman. Photo: Jan Delden/Pressens Bild

curves past Nobelparken (Nobel Park). All of Sweden's indigenous deciduous trees can be found in the park except for the mountain birch, which doesn't feel at home so far south.

Diplomatstaden (Diplomats' Town) is next to Nobelparken. This is a part of town outside the real Östermalm, and as its name suggests, it is mainly for diplomats. The ambassador of the United States lives there, amongst others. You will also find the English church, built in 1866 at Norra Bantorget and transported to Diplomatstaden in 1913.

And now we are at Gärdet, or Ladugårdsgärdet (Barn Meadow) as it is more formally called. Nowadays, Gärdet is associated mainly with the Kaknäs Tower and kite-flying shows in May. Yet for a long time the large field was a theatre of war. Both Gustav III and Karl XIV Johan used the meadow for training pitched battles. Karl Johan often used to sit in the small red fort on the slope and watch. He wanted to have a pavilion from which he could inspect the formations at the same time as he dined in comfort.

And when the manoeuvres were over for the day, he took his horse and rode back to Rosendals Castle on Djurgården.

Djurgården

*You go to Djurgården (lit. animal farm),
as in Bellman's time, to have fun. Or, as in Queen
Kristina's time, to look at the animals, both wild
and in cages. Or simply to take a walk.*

Djurgården is much larger than most people think. First of all there is Södra Djurgården, which is what most people think of as Djurgården. This is an island a little more than four kilometres long and one kilometre wide. The western part of the island, nearest the city, is taken up by Skansen, Gröna Lund, museums, restaurants, embassies and the idyllic wooden houses in Djurgårdsstaden. The rest of Södra Djurgården can be summarised in one word: park.

Then there's the part of Norra Djurgården that belongs to Gärdet. It

Riders pause on Djurgården. Photo: Johnny Palmér/Pressens Bild

Norra Djurgården is dominated by the 155-metre Kaknäs Tower, Scandinavia's second tallest building. Photo: Jeppe Wikström/Pressens Bild

lies on the northern side of Djurgårdsbrunnsviken (Djurgård Bay) with the Sjöhistoriska (Maritime History), Tekniska (Technology) and Folkens Museum (Museum of Ethnography) in a row.

The most prominent feature on Djurgården is Kaknästornet, which, at 155 metres high is the second tallest building in Scandinavia. Apart from providing an excellent vantage and boasting a restaurant and café, it is primarily used as a communications tower for radio and TV.

Finally, there is the northern part of Norra Djurgården, twice the size of the southern part.

Country Idyll

For the uninitiated, Norra Djurgården is a sort of a no-man's land, an area of unspoilt nature to the north of the inner city. It is to a great extent just that, but much money has been spent to create an open-air space where humans and nature can live together.

If you are lucky you can see deer, owls and other birds of prey, or even fish in Solfångardammen (Sun Trap Pond) at the Stora Skuggan nature and open-air centre. A number of jogging tracks and nature trails wind their way up into the woods from the pond. (There are also shower and changing-room facilities.)

Naturens Hus (Nature House), also at the open-air centre, is a sort of activities house whose purpose is to increase understanding of nature. Right beside it is a much-visited farmhouse, where children have a great time among the horses, pigs and hens.

Eco Park – the world's first national park in a city

The Eco Park is the first and still the only national park located within a metropolitan area. Its best-known tract is Södra Djurgården, but the Eco Park offers much more than this well-maintained and heavily frequented park area. The Eco Park also extends north over Gärdet, Haga Park and further on to Ulriksdal and Sörentorp. The islands of Skeppsholmen, Kastellholmen and Fjärderholmarna are also part of this trust.

Artur Hazelius – Founder of Skansen

One of the happiest days in Artur Hazelius's life was Sunday, 11 October 1891. That was the day Skansen, the world's first open-air museum, was inaugurated. Hazelius was a researcher of Nordic languages and quite a collector. On his journeys around Sweden he saw how the old rural culture was dying out as industrial society took over. He began a large collection, partly of objects of cultural and historical value, and partly of money. During ten hectic years, buildings from different parts of Sweden were imported from the countryside

Artur Hazelius. Photo: Skansen

and reconstructed on southern Djurgården. Since then, Skansen has been expanded to display a Sweden in miniature.

In May, 1995 His Majesty the King inaugurated the Eco Park and granted it perpetual protection. Today it is only possible to build in the park if construction can take place without damaging the environment, its biosystems or cultural points of interest. The Eco Park forms a landscape mosaic supporting many species of flora and fauna. Here, for instance, one can find the greatest stand of coarse oak in northern Europe and these oaks are home to the large oak-bark beetle, which can only live in these trees.

Isblad's Marsh on southern Djurgården is also noteworthy. It serves as a nesting area for the common mallard, tufted duck and coot as well as

Gröna Lund at night. Photo: Malcolm Hanes/Pressens Bild

Great Green Meadow

First a leafy garden area – whence the name Gröna Lund (Green Meadow – then, during the 1700s, a restaurant where Bellman dined regularly. Since 1883, Gröna Lund has been a fun park with a strong draw for children. There you have the roller-coaster Jetline, the round-about, the Haunted House, the Fun House and much more. Older visitors with more subdued interests can go to one of Gröna Lund's several entertainment stages. There are also numerous places to eat in the area.

for more unusual species such as the grebe, widgeon, and shoveller duck. The herons from Skansen usually can be found wading in the water, and tawny owls and sparrow hawks make their nests nearby.

But the Eco Park is not dedicated solely to the area's natural history. Many reminders of Sweden's cultural heritage are also there such as the palaces in Haga, Ulriksdal and Rosendal. The nation's oldest palace theatre "Confidencen", architect Ferdinand Boberg's gas reservoirs and other culturally important buildings in Hjorthagen make the park interesting from a cultural as well as architectural perspective.

Bellman's Terrain

Back to Södra Djurgården. Take the museum tram from Norrmalmstorg or Djurgårdsfärjan, from Gamla Stan (the Old Town) or Nybroviken. Move across to an area that makes you happy. "Stolta Stad. Jag nu glad!" (Proud town. Now I'm happy!) exclaimed Carl Michael Bellman's Mowitz as he left the bustling town for Djurgården.

There is a statue of Bellman so old that his wife and son were at its unveiling on 26 July 1829. Bellman himself had been gone for 31 years, but now the Stockholm poet was to be celebrated even more than he had been during his halcyon days under the patronage of Gustav III. Kettledrums and fanfares, choirs a-singing, soldiers and schoolchildren on parade. The king himself, Karl XIV Johan, was there.

The yearly commemoration of the statue's unveiling begins on 26 July and continues in festivities that go on for a whole week.

The Rosendal Gardens, right beside Rosendal's Castle, are a favourite place for people to take a break, not least for the quality food and drink. Now run by a group of cultivators with an emphasis on anthroposophics, the garden was the Garden Association's student school from 1861–1912. At one time there were no fewer than 443 different sorts of fruit trees there.

Another type of art – painting – can be experienced at Liljevalch´s, at Prins Eugens Waldemarsudde and Thielska Galleriet out on Blockhusudden.

The Archipelago

Laughter and fun, waltzing and rolling.
Swedes have always written songs and poems
about their most-loved landscapes, and none is more
deeply loved than the Stockholm archipelago.

Let an old archipelago boat set the pace. Start a tour out in the archipelago by first alighting at Fjäderholmarna (Feather Islands), the small archipelago just a few minutes' cruise from the centre of Stockholm. Regular tours go there from Slussen, Strömkajen and Nybroplan. The tour takes less than half an hour.

Fjäderholmarna are the first real islands of the archipelago, but the casual visitor can find all the usual amenities: restaurants, arts-and-crafts shops, theatre and an adventure playground for children. Sights worth seeing include two boat museums and a Baltic aquarium.

Ferries outward bound for the islands. Photo: Hans Nelsäter/Bildarkivet

Take a trip to Fjäderholmarna and enjoy the food and drink at Fjäderholmarnas Krog. Photo: Hans Nelsäter/Bildarkivet

Stopping off at Fjäderholmarna in order to have a good time is an old tradition. Archipelago dwellers and Stockholmers have danced, wined and partied there since the 17th century. At that time, goods and foodstuffs were brought to Stockholm either via sailing boat or rowboat. Until the end of the 19th century a visit to the Fjäderholm restaurant was always included in a journey round the town. The men of the archipelago moored their boats, full of things to be sold on the market square or direct at the quay. Live pike and perch swam around in the boat well. Baskets of eggs, bags of down and barrels of salted herring stood on the boat deck.

You can watch the sun set over Djurgården and Stockholm from the cliffs on the Fjäderholmarna islands as the archipelago boats glide by on their evening tours with passengers who love the archipelago, food and music. Herring, grilled steaks, jazz and songs: a great combination on a trip lasting a few hours through the inner archipelago. You can find information about times and ferry companies from the entertainment pages and tourist bureaux.

50

Stately Wooden Houses

On their evening tours the boats pass the Fjäderholmarna islands. They then often pass through the narrow Skurusundet (Skuru sound), where you will see a number of large wooden villas. These are known as the "merchant villas" and were built at the turn of the century as summer recreation places for merchants, district judges, company directors and factory owners.

The owners spent a few weeks each summer together with their wives, children and maids. Out on the large glass veranda the children drank juice and the wife coffee, while the man of the house sipped spiced arrack *punsch* and cognac. Today, many of the century-old houses have been beautifully restored. They are situated along the beaches of Värmdö and Lidingö and on the large islands around Vaxholm.

For those who want to go further out in the archipelago to saltier water, larger bays and smaller islands and skerries, you'll need to take a full-day cruise.

There are few places in the archipelago where fishing is the only means of livelihood. The Stockholm archipelago differs in this way from

Bullerö in Stockholm's southern archipelago. Photo: Hans Nelsäter/Bildarkivet

the Swedish west coast, the south coast and the northeast coast. The people on the large, green islands outside Stockholm have always combined fishing with a little farming.

Many of the grassy meadows and small fields are still open on the islands. This is the case on Gällnö, Svartsö and Möja. They are easily reached by scheduled boat. Here, archipelago culture is still very much alive. An expedition and walk across the islands gives you a good idea of what life in these islands was like in days gone by. The farms were small and there were few animals, but fields and meadows were plenty. Boat houses and jetties can still be found in secluded bays.

Different Faces of the Archipelago

The natural beauty of the archipelago can best be experienced by making a visit to one of its many nature reserves. Björnö, furthest out on Ingarö, is easily attainable by car, as is Gålö south of Dalarö. The only national park in the archipelago, Ängsö, is south of Norrtälje and is reachable by regular boat tours. Ask for times at the tourist bureau.

The life of a fisherman in the middle archipelago was quite different from that in the outer archipelago. Sandhamn and Landsort are two outer islands which are suitable as day-trip destinations. They are far out towards the sea and are rocky, sandy and barren. The houses there sit tightly beside one another, sheltering from easterly and northerly storms.

Hardly any grazing area for animals exists in the outer archipelago, which is why people have had difficulty providing for themselves – with one exception. Since the 16th century, various public servants – pilots, customs officers, lighthouse and telegraph operators – have made their living there. Already 500 years ago King Gustav Vasa knew that sea passage was essential to the economy of the capital and the country, and that it was impossible to navigate the archipelago's islands and skerries without help. Landsort's pilot station was first manned in 1535. The lighthouse at Landsort, the first in Sweden, was lit in 1651.

Fishermen from the middle archipelago have long had their storehouses in the outer islands. Photo: Jeppe Wikström/Pressens Bild

Fishing is still a livelihood on Huvudskär in the southern archipelago. Photo: Jeppe Wikström/Pressens Bild

Sandhamn's houses are closely packed in the lee of prevailing storms. Photo: Hans Nelsäter/Bildarkivet

Mines and Swimming

Important for Sweden, Stockholm and the archipelago, and well worth a visit, is Utö in the southern archipelago. There you will find Sweden's oldest iron-ore mine. Ore was first excavated at Utö as early as 1100. The large mine shafts, gaping open, dark and foreboding, were in use in the 18th and 19th centuries. At that time about 300 people lived in the mining village.

Archipelago lovers, bikers, campers and boaters all make their way to Utö. (There are camping sites, and bikes to rent.) There is usually an art exhibition in the old mill, and a small museum tells you about the history of the mines.

When the impoverished miners left the island in 1879, they were replaced by rich summer-resort bathers. It wasn't cold dips in the sea-water that drew them there, however, but rather warm health-giving baths, gymnastics, unusual sorts of health cures and, not least, the social life. What the resort's doctor tried to repair in the morning was often wrecked at dinner in the evening. Together with Dalarö and Furusund, Utö became one of the most popular swimming resorts in the archipelago. Many houses dating from that period remain in all three locales.

Beach and Hideout

The archipelago's best beach is at Nåttarö, south of Stockholm. It's called Stora Sand and is a gentle bay with fine white sand. Just above the beach, on a steep hill, is a shallow cave where King Gustav II's unhappy queen, Maria Eleonora, hid before desperately fleeing the kingdom (the king's death at Lutzen in 1632 had made her wretched with grief). After some years, however, she returned and now lies buried beside her beloved husband in Riddarholmskyrkan in Stockholm. (Boat to Nåttarö from Nynäshamn.)

Queen Maria Eleonora's hideaway on Nåttarö.

The Archipelago as Inspiration

The happy and restful life in the resorts attracted writers, painters and actors, and depictions of the archipelago began to appear in literature and art. August Strindberg was among the first to be inspired to write about the place, and his famous *Hemsöborna* (The People of Hemsö), published in 1887, takes Kymmendö as its motif. Strindberg stayed from time to time on Furusund and Dalarö.

After Strindberg came famous artists like Bruno Liljefors, Anders Zorn and Albert Engström. Liljefors's studio is the archipelago museum on Bullerö (boat from Stavsnäs), and Engströms's studio is a museum in Grisslehamn.

Today, about 6000 people live all the year round in the Stockholm archipelago. That isn't a lot, when you consider that the archipelago from Arholma to Landsort is 150 kilometres long, 60 kilometres wide and

Thus Sailed Zorn

In 1887 the artist Anders Zorn received the first-class medal at the World Exhibition in Paris for the oil painting *Une première*, which showed a well-fed cook and a skinny working-class boy taking the first dip of the spring. The painting was completed on Dalarö and on sailboat outings around the archipelago. It was the first time Zorn had painted cold, clean water against warm, female skin, a motif which was later to make him world famous.

Anders Zorn at sea. Photo: Pressens Bild

consists of 24,000 islands. In summer the number increases by several hundred thousand, to which can be added 150,000 small boats.

Nevertheless, it isn't difficult to find your own bays, woods and rocks. If you have plenty of time, you can hitch lifts by boat from island to island and live in tents or hostels. You can also experience the archipelago by canoe, which can be hired in a number of places. Go on discovery voyages right in the middle of the archipelago, in Stockholm or far out amongst the most distant skerries. Note, however, that a number of islands are nature preserves often with limited access during nesting season. Certain areas are also controlled by the military and access is restricted for non-Swedes.

Touring the wide Baltic ice sheets on long-distance skates. Photo: Pelle Andersson/Bildarkivet

Kayaking in the outer archipelago is an unforgettable experience. Photo: Staffan Danielsson/Bildarkivet

Lake Mälaren

*When a strong westerly wind blows,
the froth from Lake Mälaren's waves sprays over
Birger Jarl's Tower on Riddarholmen. The water colours
the worn wall a dull grey. But when the water is still, like a
looking-glass, the walls of the tower become a romantic pink:
Wild Viking sea. Smiling inland lake.*

In 1956 the archaeologist Per Lundström made the discovery of a life-time. He found a small Buddha on Helgö, not far from Drottningholm and Ekerö. Someone had dropped or hidden it in the ground at Helgö. The Buddha is one of the most unusual archaeological finds ever made in Sweden. How could an Indian Buddha have ended up in the ground on little Helgö in Mälaren so long ago?

A storm on its way over Mälaren and Riddarfjärden. Photo: Jeppe Wikström/ Pressens Bild

Ansgar's Cross at Birka was raised in 1834 in memory of the missionary Ansgar's attempt to convert the heathen Sveas. Photo: Lars Nyman/Pressens Bild

The only reasonable explanation is that traders from Mälaren had already made connections with distant India 1500 years ago, either directly or through middlemen.

There is other proof of distant trade on Helgö. Summer cottage owner Allan Hammarlund dug a hole for his flagpole and up popped a wine ladle from the eastern Mediterranean. It, too, was about 1500 years old.

Another find from the verdant Mälar island is a bishop's staff dating back 1200 years. In other words, the people around Mälaren were merchants and sailors long before the Viking period.

"The Swedes are powerful and have great fleets," wrote the Roman Tacitus just a few decades after the death of Christ. He had never visited the Svea people in the Mälar valley, but rumours must have spread.

After Helgö, it was Birka on Björkö island that became the Sveas' most important settlement. During the Viking period, between AD 800 and 1000, a thousand people lived in Birka. Archaeologists have found about 3000 graves, and new discoveries are made regularly. A new museum called "Birka, the Viking city" opened on the island during the summer of 1996. Exhibits describe life in the ancient town and the large excavations there. For information about open times and boat connections, ring ☎ 08- 560 514 45.

It was to Birka that the missionary Ansgar sailed in the middle of the 800s in his attempt to baptise the Swedish heathens.

The Mälar valley retained its importance during the whole Viking period. Nowhere in Sweden are there as many runestones as here. Most of them are on Selaön, just north of Mariefred. The runes tell about Sven, for example, who "sailed a precious ship to Domesnäs" and of a Viking who "travelled off in a manly way to England". Fröjdeborgs hill is a large burial mound on Selaön. Just beside it is a Trinity well, where women drank to become fertile.

When Olof Skötkonung (Olof the Caring) christened the Sveas and the people in the Mälar valley at the beginning of the 11th century,

The Viking museum on Birka. Photo: Jan-Eve Olsson/Riksantikvarieämbetet

Sigtuna became the most important township. He had the words "SI Dei", or "God's Sigtuna", minted on the first Swedish coin.

Castles As Museums

But let us return for a moment to Birger Jarl's Tower on Riddarholmen in the middle of Stockholm. It was Birger Jarl who established Stockholm during the 13th century, but he did not actually found the town, as legend has it and as is incorrectly written on the base of his statue on Riddarholmen.

Nor did he have Birger Jarl's Tower built, even if it does look like it dates from the Middle Ages. The tower was built in 1527 by the country's father figure, Gustav Vasa.

However, we can let the tower stand as a symbol for all the forts and castles which were built around Mälaren during the Middle Ages, the Vasa period and the Great Power period.

Today, many of them are museums open to the public. The best

Parts of Gripsholm Castle date to the 1300s, but most of the structure was built in the 1530s. Photo: Jeppe Wikström/Pressens Bild

known two are Gripsholm's Castle at Mariefred and Skokloster, representing two quite different periods and styles.

Gripsholm has its origins in the Middle Ages, and its round tower is similar to the one on Riddarholmen. Its first master was Bo Jonson Grip, one of Sweden's richest and most powerful men in the 1300s. The castle has been rebuilt and added on to many times since then, and at the end of the 18th century and the beginning of the 19th trips to Gripsholm were a popular pastime for royalty and others.

The steamer Mariefred. Photo: Jeppe Wikström/Pressens Bild

Keep Steaming

First came the steamboat to Mariefred, then the steam train on a narrow-gauge railway. There's hardly a quieter and more historic way to travel. The steamer *Mariefred* passes across Riddarfjärden, where the first Swedish steam-boats were tested in 1810. The first was called *Stockholms Häxan* (Stockholm's witch) and then came the famous paddle steamer *Amfitrite*. In Mariefred you will find the East Sörmlands railway, with 60-centimetrewide rails and conductors clad in traditional garb.

Women and Oars

Stockholm's women rowers ran regular tours to the castle. As the story goes, the strong ladies were supposed to have rowed their boats from Stockholm to Gripsholm and Mariefred in seven hours. This can't be true and must be some bluff or tall tale made up by someone with a good imagination. It is 70 kilometres from Stockholm to Gripsholm, and no woman rower ever rowed at ten kilometres an hour. King Gustav III sailed that stretch once, and it took four days. Today, the journey by steamboat takes about three hours.

Skokloster is Sweden's most magnificent baroque castle, built by General Carl Gustaf Wrangel during the latter part of the 17th century, a period of prosperity and expansion for the country. Yet it was a short era, lasting just over 50 years, and the castle was never fully decorated. All the

King Carl XVI Gustaf and Queen Silvia live at Drottningholm Palace. Also on the grounds are the beautifully maintained Drottningholm Theatre and Kina slott (China Palace), one of Europe's finest East Asian-inspired buildings. Photo: Jeppe Wikström/Pressens Bild

63

same, the treasures, some of which were fine loot and war trophies, are amongst the most valuable and interesting in the country.

When Drottningholm was rebuilt after a fire in the 1660s, the stones were not piled up for defence towers and moats. Instead, ballrooms, baroque gardens, symmetrical fountains and watery mirrors were constructed. If anyone was seen running about armed, it was because he or she was taking part in a dramatic production.

Drottningholm was Gustav III's favourite palace. Today, it is the residence of King Carl XVI Gustaf and Queen Silvia. However, the park, together with part of the palace, is open to visitors. It is easy to imagine the chitter-chatter, flirting and gossip of days gone by in the shade of the trimmed hedges and trees.

If you are travelling by car and want to experience more of the area around Lake Mälaren, you can go past Drottningholm and stop at Rastaholm, the Stockholm Sailing Ship Club harbour. Here, there are restaurants and clubhouses in fin-de-siècle style. The road then continues out towards the other larger Mälar islands, Adelsö and Munsö. There are many opportunities for swimming and enjoying the leafy Mälar landscape.

You should also visit Munsö church, one of Uppland's three "round" churches, probably built in the 1100s. At that time Estonians were ravaging the Mälar area, and women and children took shelter in the tower. The menfolk could then inundate the enemy with arrows, boiling oil and pitch.

Mälaren can also be experienced near the city. Tourists don't even have to leave central Stockholm. The first Mälar island is by Riddarfjärden, right in the middle of town – Långholmen. There you will find partying Mälaren at hand, with restaurants (including old Karlshälls gård), theatres, and bushes and copses, the last two popular with couples smitten by love.

Munsö Church was probably built in the 1100s and was, in addition the being a church, a strategic fortress lying between the established town of Sigtuna and the upstart settlement at Stockholm. Photo: Torbjörn Andersson/Pressens Bild

RESTAURANTS

*Be sure to get out and sample some of
Stockholm's restaurants; there are over 700 to choose from.
In Stockholm it's possible to have a cheap lunch at
even the flashiest and most expensive eating places that
is as tasty and well prepared as an expensive dinner.
Try the legendary Operakällaren, where Bakfickan
("the back pocket") offers a filling
meal for a bit less money.*

*The restaurants presented here have been
chosen subjectively, but all of them
are well known and liked.*

Good food in a beautiful setting. Photo: Björn Winsnes/Tiofoto

*Welcome to the table! akvarium bar & brasserie in Kungsträdgården.
Photo: Frank Chmura/Tiofoto*

Traditional Swedish

*We have chosen traditional Swedish restaurants
on the basis of their food and environment;
they range from inexpensive to exclusive.*

Den Gyldene Freden
Österlånggatan 51
☎ 08-10 90 46, 24 97 60

There are many traditional
restaurants in Gamla Stan (the
Old Town). According to a
former regular customer, Evert

Taube, the archipelago starts
right by the innermost table at
Den Gyldene Freden. Try the
traditional Swedish home
cooking or a more complex dish
such as breast of guinea-fowl
with sea crayfish.

Stadshuskällaren
Stadshuset, Kungsholmen
☎ 08-650 54 54

Stockholm's elegant City Hall, inaugurated in 1923, has become one of the city's great tourist attractions. The atmosphere in the basement restaurant is also very distinguished. You can have the whole Nobel menu, but it will cost you. There's a cheaper alternative for those who haven't yet received a Nobel Prize.

Källaren Diana
Brunnsgränd 2
☎ 08-10 73 10

One of Gamla Stan's cellar restaurants. The "archipelago" boat filled with white herring, Baltic herring and other types of fish is famous. Källaren Diana has a long tradition of serving well-prepared home cooking. Fowl often features on the menu.

Lidingöbro Värdshus
Kaknäsvägen 62–72
☎ 08-662 06 94

The best time to go to Lidingöbro is on a warm summer evening. It is on Norra Djurgården, right by the water. The pavilion gives it the feeling of being an out-of-town restaurant. When the weather permits, the grill moves outdoors.

Operakällaren
Operahuset
Dining room and veranda
☎ 08-676 58 01,
Café Opera ☎ 08-676 58 07,
Bakfickan ☎ 08-676 58 09,
Bar ☎ 08-676 58 08

Stockholm's showcase restaurant, or restaurants, since there are several under the same roof. Here you eat in a distinguished, expensive and international setting in the dining room or inexpensively in the Bar and Bakfickan. Café Opera is also a nightclub.

In Gamla Stan's Järntorget one can visit the classic restaurant Den Gyldene Freden. Since the 1700's it has been a meeting place for many Stockholm poets. Photo: Bengt af Geijerstam/Bildhuset

Restaurang Gondolen
Stadsgården 6
☎ 08-641 70 90

Unquestionably the best view in
Stockholm. As a guest you float,
as if in a flying gondola, right
over Slussen between Saltsjön
and Mälaren. Below lie Gamla
Stan and Södermalm.

Restaurant Pelikan
Blekingegatan 40
☎ 08-743 06 95

This is what most restaurants
looked like on Söder 60 years ago.
Busy, smoky and a little grubby,
the staff dressed in black and
white. There isn't a more genuine
Stockholm atmosphere to be
found anywhere.

Ulriksdals Wärdshus
Solna
☎ 08-85 08 15

Beautiful setting and excellent
food, and if not exactly first-class,
the service is friendly and polite.
One of the best restaurants in
Stockholm.

Wärdshuset Godthem
Rosendalsvägen 9, Djurgården
☎ 08-661 07 22

Outdoor restaurant with an
atmosphere from the 1897
Stockholm Exhibition. Godthem
is on Djurgården, right after
Djurgårdsbron and within
walking distance from the city
centre. The steaks are famous.

Zum Franziskaner
Skeppsbron 44
☎ 08-411 83 30

A place for smoked herring,
Janzon (herring and potato
casserole) and "pytt i panna"
(diced potatoes and meat fried
up in a pan), in other words,
good value Swedish home
cooking. Jugendstil decor;
benches and tables as in a
German beer garden.

Meat and Grills

*Meat dishes are served
in most of the restaurants in Stockholm.
We have selected what we think are some of the best,
where the chefs know how to choose a piece of cured, hanged
beef and cook it properly on the stove or grill.*

Brasserie Vau-de-Ville
Hamngatan 17
☎ 08-611 25 22

You can hardly find a more cent-
rally located restaurant. Vau-de-
Ville is in the corner of Norrmalmstorg square. The sausage
and sauerkraut in the café are to
be recommended. The smarter
area is a little on the French side.

Butlers
Rörstrandsgatan 11
☎ 08-32 18 23

Carl Butler taught the Swedes
how to prepare good, simple food
with the help of a cookbook full
of pictures. Lamb, together with
other simple, quality food, has
since been served at this little
restaurant in Vasastan.

Meat and fowl prepared with care. Photo: Björn Winsnes/Tiofoto

Grodan

Grev Turegatan 16
☎ 08-679 61 00

One of the best meeting places in town, so they say. This means that people who want to see and be seen go to Grodan. Game and French cuisine. Outdoor service.

Heartbreak Hotel

Kungsgatan 18
☎ 08-10 73 73

If you name a restaurant after an old Elvis song, it's got to suit the name. Spare ribs, American burgers, a great lunch salad buffet, and walls covered with rock 'n' roll paraphernalia.

L'escargot Restaurant

Scheelegatan 8
☎ 08-650 98 09

You can hardly get nearer to Paris in Stockholm. Very French and elegant on the first floor. Less elegant but still French and popular on the ground floor.

La Brochette

Storgatan 27
☎ 08-662 20 00

Right in the middle of the advertising agency district. This means quick, good lunches. French menu, as the name implies.

Nils-Emil Restaurang

Folkungagatan 12
☎ 08-640 72 09
Closed Jul–Aug

Finest on Söder, and popular. Home fare dominates. Meat wrapped in cabbage (kåldolmar) has character, and Baltic herring is given a good showing.

Restaurang Morellen

Bergsgatan 33
☎ 08-651 36 60

The newspapers and restaurant guides can't all be wrong. Morellen is hailed as one of the best lunch and local restaurants in Stockholm. Everything is quite squashed here around the herring rissoles with currant sauce and horseradish. One main topic of conversation is how it is possible to prepare such a variety of dishes in such a small kitchen!

Seafood Restaurants

The number of Stockholm restaurants that specialise in fish is relatively low for a seaside city, but they are of excellent quality. Specialities include herring, especially the tender Baltic variety and pike-perch, which can be caught in both the Baltic and the inland lakes. "International" fish such as salmon and sole are also widely available.

akvarium bar and brasserie
Kungsträdgården
☎ 08-10 06 26

Shellfish dishes are scribbled down on a blackboard. The aquarium is by Kungsträdgården and has an exciting, youthful decor. You can also have sandwiches and soups.

Enjoy good salmon. Photo: Björn Winsnes/Tiofoto

Gerda's Fisk & Kräfthandel
Östermalms saluhall
☎ 08-662 10 54

Östermalm's food hall is a place for all the senses. According to the poet Lars Forssell, the place smells of cod, shellfish and the 19th century. This and a lot more can be found at Gerda Johansson, one of the hall's twenty traders. You can have fish dishes for lunch or as an early dinner – the food hall closes at 18.00.

Le bistro de Wasahof
Dalagatan 46
☎ 08-32 34 40

Oysters are an ideal entrée. They are not heavy, so you can eat many. The better class of cook-books from the last century recommended 144 per person. At Wasahof the oysters are cheap, though maybe not as cheap as in those days. There are also many delicious, French-inspired dishes to choose from.

Restaurang Kajplats 9
Norr Mälarstrand, Kajplats 9
☎ 08-652 45 45

Kajplats 9 is on the quay, with the water of Riddarfjärden splashing about the veranda. Well prepared fresh- and salt-water fish are served, as well as shellfish.

Sturehof
Stureplan
☎ 08-679 87 50

An old fish restaurant in the middle of town with a traditional menu. Turbot with butter and horse-radish. The pub part is nearest the street, but once past it you are in the quiet atmosphere of the fish restaurant.

Wedholms Fiskrestaurang
Nybrokajen 17
☎ 08-611 78 74

Perhaps the most distinguished fish restaurant in Stockholm, but the bill need not be unreasonably high if you choose from among the cheaper fish. For example, try the plaice meunière.

Dancing and Music

The entertainment pages of the newspapers give details about which performers and orchestras will be playing in the city's nightclubs and discothèques. Note that the minimum age for entry is often 23.

Berns' Salonger
Berzelii Park
☎ 08-614 07 20

Stockholm's classic entertainment temple. Everyone and everything is there beneath magnificent cutglass chandeliers. Food, bars, dancing and shows.

Börsen
Jakobsgatan 6
☎ 08-787 85 00

You go to Börsen more to see the show and to dance than to eat. All the top musicians perform at Börsen, and tickets must be booked in advance.

The large outdoor veranda at Berns' is a magnet for Stockholmers and tourists alike. Photo: Frank Chmura/Tiofoto

Stampen in Gamla Stan is a rendezvous for jazz lovers. Photo: Chad Ehlers/Tiofoto

Engelen and Kolingen

Kornhamnstorg 59 B
☎ 08-20 10 92, 611 62 00

Engelen calls itself a music pub. Food, beer and music, ranging from rock to Dixieland and blues. If you want to go on after midnight you need to go down one floor to Kolingen, which closes at 03.00.

Göta Källare

Folkungagatan 45, on the subway platform level at Medborgarplatsen
☎ 08-642 08 28, 640 19 56

The big dance hall on Södermalm. Often with live music played by the best Swedish dance bands. Disco from time to time.

Mosebacke Etablissement

Mosebacke Torg 3
☎ 08-641 90 20, 640 46 60

On the top of Söder. Mosebacke is frequented by shaggy bards there to have a beer, actors dressed in black talking about their latest performance and ordinary Söder dwellers listening to music and watching the cabaret. On some summer evenings there is dancing on the terrace.

Stampen

Stora Nygatan 5
☎ 08-20 57 93, 20 57 86

The smoky epicentre of Dixieland in Stockholm. At Stampen you drink beer and tap time with your feet.

Wallmans Salonger

Teatergatan 3
☎ 08-611 66 22

The waiters and waitresses at Wallmans should be able to entertain, sing, enchant and show off, as well as serve food. And they can!

Pubs

Meeting at pubs has become popular in Stockholm in recent years. Many streets have several pubs on Söder. Irish pubs have become especially popular. Simple meals as well as beer are served.

Beefeater Inn
Götgatan 11
☎ 08-641 42 72

Scottish. Götgatsbacken is the area of Stockholm most packed with pubs, but this is the only one where the staff wear kilts.

Black & Brown Inn
Hornsgatan 50 B
☎ 08-644 82 80

British. Prefers to be called public house and not just pub. In addition to real ale and many other types of beer, customers can choose from among 24 types of whisky.

Limerick
Tegnérgatan 10
☎ 08-673 43 98

Irish. Among the Irish pubs that have opened in recent years in Stockholm, the Limerick pub has been most successful. Here, you can get Irish beer, Irish whisky, Irish music (live and recorded) and Irish staff.

Löwenbräu
Fridhemsplan 29
☎ 08-653 97 70

German. More of a beer cellar than a pub. A classic from the press district around Klara, which has had a new start with the recent pub culture. Yet it still retains its atmosphere. It moved from Klara about the same time as the newspapers Dagens Nyheter and Expressen and is now at Fridhemsplan on Kungsholmen.

Norra Brunn
Surbrunnsgatan 33
☎ 08-16 61 80

Here, you can get beer on tap, in bottles (70 types) and beer in a half-metre glass. Stand-up comedy on certain days as well as other entertainment.

SHOPS AND DEPARTMENT STORES

Many people travel to Stockholm just for the shops.
Some people know what they want before they set out.
Others stroll around, buying on spur-of-the-moment
decisions. Even so, hints are usually welcome, so here are
a few – subjectively chosen – suggestions for places to shop in
Stockholm. If you're on the look out for something out of
the ordinary, look under "Specialist shops".

Shopping hours are normally 09.30–18.00 on weekdays and
09.30–14.00 on Saturdays. Department stores are usually
open until 19.00 on weekdays, 17.00 on Saturdays
and from 12.00 to 16.00 on Sundays.

Books

The biggest bookshop in town – *Akademibokhandeln,* on the corner of Regeringsgatan and Mäster Samuelsgatan – sells everything from paperbacks to lavish coffee-table books on a whole range of subjects. Akademibokhandeln has most topics covered, in Swedish, English and other languages. *NK* also has a sizeable book department, while *Åhléns* is a lower-priced alternative. Bookworms looking for old treasures should make their way to *Rönnells* (Birger Jarlsgatan 32). Drottninggatan, north of Olof Palmes Gata, also has a number of antiquarian booksellers where precious finds can be made. Gamla Stan has a pearl, *Aspingtons* (Västerlånggatan 54); very Swedish, but German books as well as fine art prints are also stocked. One floor up in Sweden House is the *Sweden Bookshop,* with a selection of books about Sweden in various languages.

Ejes on Gärdet makes their own chocolate confections.
Photo: Jan Düsing /Pressens Bild

Furniture

Shoppers looking for reasonably priced furnishings or furniture could take a bus (free)Regeringsgatan 13 to *IKEA* (at Kungens Kurva, in the suburb of Skärholmen). True home interior devotees will enjoy looking round Stockholm's many shops in this field, luxury and budget priced, established and up-and-coming. *Nordiska Galleriet* (Nybrogatan 11) is modern, expensive, exquisite. *Svenskt Tenn* (Strandvägen) is classically Swedish: cretonnes by Josef Frank. Furniture by *Carl Malmsten* (Strandvägen 5b), expensive. *Galleri Asplund* (Sibyllegatan 31): small, discriminating, modern Swedish style. *House* (Odengatan 79 and several other addresses in Stockholm) is a delightful blend of styles – kitsch, Gustavian and modern. *Klara* (Birger Jarlsgatan 34) is simple, low priced, mixed style. *R.O.O.M* (Alströmergatan 20) is new, big and stocks a mixture of styles.

Arts, Crafts and Glassware

Swedish glass is world famous. Well-known Stockholm shops selling glass include *Galleri Orrefors* (Grevgatan 1), with a permanent exhibition of superb quality. Luxurious, and not to be missed. *Svenskt Glas* (Birger Jarlsgatan 8), features modern glassware from Reijmyre and Kosta Boda. *The Erik Höglund Gallery,* on the "hump" on Hornsgatan, Södermalm, is the artist's own showcase for his clear, colourful creations. But the most-visited place for buying glassware in Stockholm is the *NK* department store, one floor down from the main level.

High-quality Swedish craft products are found at *Hemslöjden* (Sveavägen 44), and *Konsthantverkarna* (Mäster Samuelsgatan 2). Look for the *Blås & Knåda* (ceramics and glass) and *Metallum* (silver and other metals) galleries on the Hornsgatan hump. Danish silver and porcelain of the highest quality are to be found at *Georg Jensen* (Birger Jarlsgatan 13). *Nutida Svenska Silver* (Arsenalgatan 3) displays and sells innovative silver jewellery.

Tiogruppen (Götgatan 25) is well known for its colourful fabrics and ceramics. More Swedish style, but at the same time modern, are the

ceramics. More Swedish style, but at the same time modern, are the fabrics produced at Klässbols Linneväveri, of Värmland, and sold at *Maja Cronsjö's* shop (Svartmangatan 19, Gamla Stan).

Games and Hobbies

Stor&Liten (Gallerian, Hamngatan) is a supermarket for toys and games. The upper floor has a bewildering array of amusements – construction kits, rattles, dolls, monsters and Lego sets – while the lower floor is given over to video games. The atmosphere is calmer at *Leka Samman* (Horns-gatan 50 B). Beauty and sturdiness are the criteria for toys in this small, unusual shop. The same is true of *Bulleribock* (Sveavägen 104), which stocks fine-quality toys in wood and other natural materials. If you are looking for a practical joke, visit *Butterick's* (Drottninggatan 57). Whoopee cushions, stink bombs, false beards, conjuring tricks are all found here along with costumes and fancy dress. Connoisseur hobbyists should make their way to *Eskader* (Gumshornsgatan 8, Östermalm), a shop famous for model railways, steam engines, model ships and military models. All true to scale, of course. Gallerian (Hamngatan) has another well-stocked hobby shop, *Wentzels Hobby.*

Fashion

The art of buying – or window shopping for – clothes is best practised in Biblioteksgatan (exclusive), Hamngatan (varied styles) or Drottningga-tan (fashion for the young). Discriminating shoppers with money to spend should head for Sturegallerian and Östermalm – Nybrogatan, Grev Turegatan and Humlegårdsgatan. Östermalm also has several second-hand clothes shops: *Cattis* and *Två tre gånger* (Linnégatan 33–34), *Tant Gredelins Garderob* (Karlavägen 72) and *Keps Second Hand* (Artillerigatan 83), to name a few.

The fashion hungry shouldn't miss *NK Trend,* two floors up in the department store. There, young Swedish fashion designers prove that Sweden can also make a contribution on the international scene. *Clark's Case* (Hornsgatan 68) is a shop of a slightly different type, with a mixture of fashion and interior design, second-hand and new.

Söderhallarna at Medborgarplatsen on Söder. Photo: Frank Chmura/ Tiofoto

Market Halls

Stockholm has three market halls, all of which have a mixture of stalls selling delicatessen products, plants and flowers, fresh meat and fish, as well as plenty of snack bars.

Östermalmshallen is Stockholm's answer to Les Halles in Paris. Varied and crowded, but at the same time courteous and calm. *Hötorgshallen,* down the escalator at Hötorget, has a wonderful blend of southern European and Swedish produce, snack bars and small restaurants. Bustling, fragrant and exotic. *Söderhallarna* (Medborgarplatsen, Södermalm) is the newcomer, opened in 1992. Smaller than the other market halls, but the same mixture.

Specialist Shops

Cities have all kinds of shops. In some, just going in and soaking up the atmosphere is an experience in itself. And it's Stockholm's specialist shops that give the city a special flavour. At *Æter & Essencefabriken* (Wallingatan 14) you can choose from 200 different spices in a milieu that has stayed the same for four generations. Opened in 1889, the shop is still owned by the Lilieblad family, and the interior has remained largely unchanged. *Sibyllans Kaffe o. Tehandel* (Sibyllegatan 35) is another family-owned shop with a history. Enjoy the aroma of freshly ground coffee, ask for tips about making up your own selection or choose a classic blend. Tea lovers on Södermalm go to the *Tea Centre,* on the hump on Hornsgatan, to taste and choose among teas from all over the world. Visitors to *Fartygsmagasinet* (Österlånggatan 19, Gamla Stan), a shop selling relics from boats and ships, are greeted by the smell of marlines, red lead and the sea.

Department Stores/Shopping Malls

NK (Hamngatan 18–20) is Stockholm's most international department store. *Åhléns* (Klarabergsgatan 50/Drottninggatan) is similar to NK, but is lower priced. Åhléns has a very well stocked food department.

Gallerian (Hamngatan 37) is an arcade that houses more than 40 shops of various kinds. Similar, although more chic, is *StureGallerian* (Stureplan). *PUB* (Hötorget/Drottninggatan 72) is another gallery-style shopping area that combines a wide assortment of stores.

The NK department store. Photo: Malcolm Hanes/Pressens Bild

MUSEUMS AND SIGHTS

*Many people love museums, while others simply find them
dusty and dull. People in the second category should try again
– in Stockholm alone, there are some 70 museums
of every imaginable sort.*

Museums in and near Stockholm, which cater to nearly every possible
interest, are listed and described below.

Opening hours vary, but as is standard international practice, most close
on Mondays. However, there are some important exceptions to that rule,
including the Royal Palace and the Vasa Museum. Entry charges vary up
to a maximum of 65 kronor for adults. Children and pensioners normally go in for half price.

BUS = nearest bus line
SUBWAY = nearest underground (Tunnelbana) station
RAIL = nearest commuter train station

*Judith Leyster (1609–1660), "Boy blowing a flute". Photo: National-
museum/Statens Konstmuseer, Stockholm*

Albert Engström Museums

Grisslehamn. BUS 637 from Tekniska Högskolan.
☎ 0175-308 90
Open: 6/5–5/6, 26/8–1/10, weekends 12.00–15.00; 10/6–20/8 daily 11.00–16.00; closed Midsummer Eve.

The Albert Engström Museums consist of Engström's studio and house at Grisslehamn. The studio, out near the sea, has a display of photographs and drawings, and Engström's easel – complete with an unfinished drawing – is set up by the window. Albert Engström's home is shown complete with original furnishings and decor.

K.A. Almgrens Silkweaving Museum

Repslagargatan 15, SUBWAY Slussen.
☎ 08-642 56 16
Open: Group tours are available and should be booked in advance. Times: 10.00, 11.30, 14.00, 14.30, 15.00, 18.00, 19.30; Mon–Fri 08.00–17.00. Closed weekends.

An industrial landmark, the Silkweaving Museum has existed since 1833 and has been located at its present address since the 1840s. Among its displays is a collection of drawings of patrons. Silk cloth has been woven here for numerous important figures and institutions, and a selection of fabrics can be seen along with the famed Almgrean shawls. Today's production is used by the Army Museum, the Royal Collections and the Royal Patriotic Association. Function room and gift store.

Aquaria–Water Museum

Falkenbergsgatan 2, Djurgården
BUS 44, 47; tram and ferry services.
☎ 08-660 49 40
Open: Jun–Aug, daily 10.00–18.00; Sep–May, Tue–Sun 10.00–16.30.

Aquaria is a new type of museum. Through the application of technology, visitors experience night and day in a tropical rain forest, see a variety of fish and frogs and listen to all the sounds of that special environment. Moving on, visitors arrive at "the sea", with aquariums of sharks, moray eels and living coral. Restaurant.

Swedish Museum of Architecture

Skeppsholmen, SUBWAY Kungsträdgården BUS 65.
☎ 08-463 05 00
Open: 1/9–31/5 Tue 11.00–18.00, Wed–Sun 11.00–16.00, 1/6–31/8 Tue 11.00–20.00, Wed–Sun 11.00–17.00.

Sweden's only architectural museum is located in Stockholm. The museum is now going through a process of change that will culminate with the inauguration of a new location in 1998 where a permanent exhibition will be created. Increased activity will also be focused on the archive and library. An exhibition entitled "Modern Museums" is being shown in the present location until winter 1997. The museum's archive with approximately one million plans and sketches, 400,000 photos and numerous models and books is open for visitors. Bookstore and film salon.

The Bellman Museum

Stora Henriksvik, Långholmen Island (see page 8).

Bergian Botanical Gardens

Frescati, SUBWAY Universitetet, BUS 540, 40 or RAIL Frescati.
☎ 08-5789 0015, 16 28 53, 15 65 45
Open: Edvard Anderson's Mediterranean Greenhouse,

Giant lily pad in the Victoria Greenhouse of the Bergian Gardens. Photo: Hans Nelsäter/Bildarkivet

daily 11.00–17.00; Victoria Greenhouse, 1/5–30/9, daily 11.00–17.00.

Victoria is the name given to a huge water lily that flowers in the greenhouse of the same name. The plant's leaves grow up to 2.5 metres in diameter. A wide variety of plants can be seen at the Bergian Botanical Gardens north of the city centre. In the greenhouse you'll find cork oak, olive trees and Mediterranean herbs and spices growing. A stroll in the park is also recommended.

Museum of Biology

Djurgården, BUS 44, 47; tram and ferry.
☎ 08-442 82 15
Open: 1/10–31/3, Tue–Sun 10.00–15.00; 1/4–30/9, daily 10.00–16.00.

The Museum of Biology, a small brown building next to the Hazelius entrance to Skansen, was completed in 1893 for the Stockholm Exhibition in 1897. Its style is pure Old Norse. The museum displays a range of stuffed animals, common and

Interior from the Museum of Biology. Photo: Bengt af Geijerstam/Bildhuset

not so common, against a background of panoramas painted by Bruno Liljefors. The Museum of Biology was the first in the world to use the idea of showing animals in their natural habitats.

The Blockmaker's House
Stigbergsgatan 21, BUS 46, 48, 53.
☎ 08-700 05 00
Open: Ring for further information.
At his house on Stigbergsgatan, Södermalm, Andersson the blockmaker made block and tackle rigs for sailing ships in the early 1900s. The house, now a museum, shows a typical interior from that era. The building itself dates from the early 18th century.

Cosmonova
Swedish Museum of Natural History, Frescativägen 40.
SUBWAY Universitetet, BUS 40, 540
☎ 08-666 40 00, 666 51 30 (ticket office)
Open: Film shows on the hour, morning to evening.

Cosmonova, an omnitheatre with a modern planetarium/cinema of vast proportions, is a very popular attraction. Films on subjects in the field of popular natural science are shown on a dome-shaped screen. The sensation of being part of the scene – as it unfolds above you and around you – is almost real.

Dalarö Customs Museum
Tullhuset, Dalarö. BUS 839 from Haninge Centrum.
☎ 08-501 511 16
Open: Jun–Aug, Tue–Sun 11.00–16.00; closed Midsummer Eve. Other visits by arrangement.

Idyllic Dalarö is situated in the south of Stockholm's archipelago. The museum is accommodated in Dalarö's Customs House, built in 1788. Exhibits illustrate the long history of the customs organisation in Sweden, how contraband was smuggled in olden times and how spirits were smuggled between the wars. Another display tells of today's illegal trade in narcotics.

Museum of Dance
Barnhusgatan 14, Folkets hus.
SUBWAY T-Centralen, BUS 47, 69, 53.
☎ 08-10 82 43
Open: Tue–Sun 12.00–16.00.
Two exhibitions per year.

The only one of its type in the world, the Museum of Dance tells the story of dance of all kinds, although mainly European, in a variety of settings. Stage design sketches, works of art, stage models, costumes, masks, musical instruments. Major exhibitions on Swedish and Russian ballet, modern dance and folk dance.

Drottningholm Palace Theatre and Museum of Theatre

Drottningholm. SUBWAY Brommaplan, then BUS 301–323.
☎ 08-759 04 06
Open: Daily, 1/5–31/8 12.00–16.30, 1/ 9–30/9 13.00–15.30.

Drottningholm Palace, the residence of King Carl XVI Gustaf and Queen Silvia, has the world's best preserved 18th-century theatre – including the original scenery – still in use. An exhibition showing the development of scenery art is located in Hertig Carls Pavilion next to the theatre.

Carl Eldh's Studio Museum

Lögebodavägen 10. SUBWAY Odenplan, then to BUS 40, 46, 52, 53.
☎ 08-612 65 60
Open: 1/6–31/8, Tue–Sun 12.00–16.00; May and Sep weekends 12.00–16.00; Apr and Oct, Sun 12.00–16.00; Nov–Mar by appointment.

Carl Eldh's sculpting studio is located in Bellevue Park surrounded by a beautiful garden. The building was designed by Ragnar Östberg and erected in 1919, and it was here that Carl Eldh lived and worked until his death in 1954. Since that time the studio has been left largely undisturbed; it contains a significant portion of Eldh's work, including drafts, sketches and casting moulds.

The Butterfly and Bird House

Haga Garden, Hagaparken. BUS 515 from Odenplan.
☎ 08-730 39 81
Open: Summer, Tue–Fri 10.00–16.00, weekends 11.00–17.30; winter, Tue–Fri 10.00–15.00, weekends 11.00–16.00.
Sweden's first tropical butterfly and bird house is situated in beautiful Hagaparken, north of the city centre. Beautiful butterflies and birds fly free in the 2000-square-metre tropical forest. Plans are underway to build a new Insect House with an evolutionary theme.

A visit to the Butterfly House in Haga Park. Photo: Jack Mikrut/ Pressens Bild

National Museum of Ethnography

Djurgårdsbrunnsvägen 34, BUS 69.
☎ 08-666 50 00
Open: Tue–Fri 11.00–16.00, Wed 11.00–20.00, weekends 12.00–17.00.

Get an insight into life outside Europe at the National Museum of Ethnography. With 150,000 objects from Africa, Asia, the Americas, Oceania and Australia the museum's exhibits take up humanity's universal problems and how they are solved by various cultures around the world. The Japanese tea house is open for ceremonies during summer months and the Babajan Ethno-bar serves its world buffet all year round.

The Gold Room, Museum of National Antiquities

(see page 92)

The Hallwyl Museum (Hallwylska Museet)

Hamngatan 4. SUBWAY Öster-malmstorg, Birger Jarlsgatan exit or BUS 47, 46, 62.
☎ 08-666 44 99
Open: 15/8–25/6, Tue–Sun 12.00–16.00; 26/6–15/8, daily 11.00–16.00. Tours on the hour.

In the middle of the city lies this palatial home from the turn of the 20th century. The building, steeped in splendour and opulence, was donated to the nation after the death of the Countess Wilhelmina von Hallwyl in 1930. Salons and rooms are furnished and decorated in the styles of different epochs, including 17th century Dutch painting, European porcelain and Chinese ceramics. Summer evening concerts are highly appreciated events.

Museum of National Antiquities

Narvavägen 13–17. SUBWAY Karlaplan Östermalmstorg, BUS 44, 47, 56, 69, 76.
☎ 08-783 94 00
Open: Tue–Sun 11.00–17.00; winter also Thu 17.00–20.00.

Housing one of Sweden's richest collections of objects from the Stone Age to the present, this is also one of the oldest museums in the world, with activities dating to the 1570s. The exceptional Viking displays include gold and silver treasures in the magnificent Gold Room. "The bright Dark Ages", 2000 sq. metres of exhibits describing the Swedish Medieval Period will open in Spring 1997. Other services include refreshments, a gift shop and a cinema.

Jewish Museum

Hälsingegatan 2. SUBWAY Odenplan, BUS 47
☎ 08-31 01 43
Open: Wed, Sun 12.00–16.00; 15/6–15/8, Mon, Tue, Thu 12–16.

The museum depicts Jewish integration into Swedish society and the Jewish contribution to Swedish culture, industry and trade. The exhibition begins in 1774, the year Aaron Isaac arrived as the first Jew allowed to settle in Sweden. A permanent exhibition on the Holocaust is also included.

Junibacken

Galärparken, Djurgården, BUS 44, 47, tram, ferry.
☎ 08-660 06 00 (information), tickets 077-170 70 70
Open: Daily 10.00–18.00.

A fanciful and fascinating house where you travel by train through Astrid Lindgren's storybook world. Includes a playhouse for children and an old-time café. Multimedia room and bookstore with music, CD ROM diskettes and videotapes.

Stockholm Cultural Centre (Kulturhuset)

Sergels Torg 3 SUBWAY T-Centralen, BUS 47, 52, 59, 65.
☎ 08-700 01 00
Open: Tue–Fri from 11.00; Sat–Sun from 12.00.

A monolithic concrete and glass structure, the centre has cultural activities and exhibitions on several floors. The building is representative of the architectural style that typified the rapid renovation of the city centre during the 1960s and 1970s. The

Kulturhuset is a centre for contemporary culture offering exhibitions, reading rooms, theatre and restaurants. Photo: Nina Ericson/Bildhuset

centre serves as a living cultural centre with theatre, dance, concerts and regular exhibitions of paintings, sculpture, architecture, crafts, design, photography, video etc. It is also possible to listen to music and to borrow newspapers and books in various languages.

Kaknäs Tower (Kaknästornet)

Kaknäsvägen, Norra Djurgården. BUS 69.
☎ 08-789 24 35
Open: Summer 9.00–22.00; winter 10.00–21.00.

The second tallest observation tower in Scandinavia (155 metres), Kaknäs Tower offers a spectacular 360-degree view of Stockholm as well as a restaurant, café, tourist office and souvenir shop. The tower also operates as a relay station for radio and TV.

Gustavsberg Centre of Ceramics

Odelbergs väg 5 B, Gustavsberg.
BUS 424–440 from Slussen.
☎ 08-570 356 58
Open: Mon–Fri 10.00–17.00, Sat 10.00–15.00, Sun 11.00–15.00.

The Centre displays the old factory's production of household porcelain and art objects dating from the company's inception in 1825 to the present. There is also a painting studio with demonstrations and "do-it-yourself" activities as well as a workshop with ceramicist Lisa Larsson and her helpers.

The Royal Palace
Gamla Stan. SUBWAY Gamla Stan, BUS 43, 46, 55, 59, 76.
☎ 08-402 61 30

Stockholm's Royal Palace is unique in that very large parts of the building are open to the public. As many as six museums are based in the palace.

The Gustav III Museum of Antiquities
☎ 08-402 60 00
Open: 1/6–31/8, daily 10.00–16.00.

A collection of antique marble statues that Gustav III sent back to Sweden during a visit to Italy are displayed in beautiful settings with views over Logården, on the east side of the palace. This is Sweden's oldest official museum in its original location and with its original interior. The museum's rooms have recently received extensive renovations and are now open to the public.

The Royal Armoury
☎ 08-666 44 75 (-85 on weekends and holidays), 666 44 79 (answering machine).
Open: Tue–Sun 11.00–16.00; 1/5–31/8, also Mon 11.00–16.00.

The oldest museum in Sweden (1628). Magnificent state coaches, suits of armour, hunting weapons, coronation costumes, masquerade costumes and much more. The museum has a children's association called Riddarklubben (Knight's Club) that has become very popular.

Representation Floors
☎ 08-402 61 30
Open: 1/9–31/5, Tue–Sun 12.00–15.00; 1/6–31/8, Mon–Sun 10.00–16.00.

Sumptuous rooms and halls: the Bernadotte floor with Lovisa Ulrika's audience room, guest floors and celebration halls with Karl XI's gallery, White Sea, the Parade bedroom, and more.

The Treasury
☎ 08-402 61 30
Open: 1/9–31/5, Tue–Sun 12.00–15.00; 1/6–31/8, daily 10.00–16.00.

The White Sea at Stockholm's palace. Photo: Alexis Daflos/ Kungl. Husgerådskammaren

Here, Sweden's regalia, including the oldest – Gustav Vasa's two swords of state – may be seen. Other treasures include the crowns of kings and princes, sceptres and orbs.

Royal Chapel
☎ 08-402 61 30
Open: Jun–Aug, Mon–Sat 10.00–16.00, Sun 12.00–16.00; service all year round at 11.00 every Sunday and public holiday.

Originally a baroque building, rococo decorations were added by Carl Hårleman in 1754. Painted ceilings and sculptural ornamentation were created by Swedish and French artists. The chapel serves as the church of the Royal Parish, but is also open to the public, including religious services.

Toy Museum
Mariatorget 1. SUBWAY Mariatorget, BUS 43, 55, 75.
☎ 08-641 61 00
Open: Tue–Fri 10.00–16.00, weekends 12.00–16.00.
Thousands of toys and models are displayed on five floors. A bonanza for toy lovers of any age. Children's theatre.

Liljevalch's Art Gallery
Djurgårdsvägen 60. BUS 44, 47; also tram or ferry.
☎ 08-14 46 35, 662 05 09
Open: During exhibitions Tue– Sun 11.00–17.00, Tue–Thu to

20.00. The Gallery is closed for reconstruction 1/4–31/12 1997.

Many Swedish artists have found fame at Liljevalch's spring salon. Every year, a jury chooses from around 7000 contributions and 300–400 works are exhibited for a month during February and March and for two months afterward. Liljevalch's concentrates mainly on modern art, but art and crafts from earlier periods are also displayed. Liljevalch's is situated between the Nordiska museet (Nordic Museum) and the Gröna Lund amusement park on Djurgården. A much-appreciated café, Blå Porten, is next door.

The Puppet Museum

Brunnsgatan 6. SUBWAY Östermalmstorg or Hötorget, BUS 41, 46, 51.
☎ 08-10 30 61
Open: Tue–Sun 13.00–16.00; closed for the summer 1/6–31/7.

See the art of puppet theatre in all its many forms, both with regard to role technique and artistic interpretation. Swedish and foreign puppets, with a large collection from Asia.

Mediterranean Museum

Fredsgatan 2. SUBWAY Kungs-trädgården, BUS 62, 65.
☎ 08-783 94 10
Open: Tue 11.00– 21.00, Wed–Sun 11.00–16.00.

In this museum you can find ancient marble sculptures, Greek vases, Etruscan tomb gifts, Greek and Roman gold jewellery, ancient Cypriot votive sculptures, Islamic art and Egyptian mummies. The newly opened Near Eastern exhibit includes ancient architecture and sculpture in a Renaissance inspired interior. Café and museum shop.

Museum of the Medieval Stockholm

Strömparterren, Helgeands-holmen, Norrbro. SUBWAY Kungsträdgården, BUS 43, 62.
☎ 08-700 05 93, bookings 20 61 68
Open: 1/9–30/6 Tue and Thu–Sun 11.00–16.00, Wed 11.00–18.00; 1/7–31/8 Tue–Thu 11.00–18.00; Fri–Mon 11.00–16.00.

The mysteries of the Middle Ages unfold before you in this underground museum on Helgeands-holmen, between Gamla Stan and the modern city centre. When excavations for an underground car park for Sweden's Parliament

The Museum of the Medieval Stockholm on Helgeandsholmen provides a breathtakingly realistic look at life in Stockholm during the 15th century. Photo: Lars Dahlström/Tiofoto

began in the 1970s, ruins and skulls dating from the Middle Ages were found. This is now one of Stockholm's more evocative museums, with low lighting and sounds from the 15th-century town.

The Milles Museum (Millesgården)

Carl Milles väg 2, Lidingö. SUBWAY Ropsten, then RAIL to Torsvik or BUS 201–202, 204–206, 212.
☎ 08-731 50 60
Open: May–Sept, daily 10.00– 17.00; Oct–April, Sun 12.00–16.00.

The lower terrace of Millesgården with various sculptures by Carl Milles including God's hand and the musical angels. Photo: Lars Dahlström/ Tiofoto

The Milles Museum is located in sculptor Carl Milles's home on Lidingö and the view over Stockholm from the beautiful terraces is exceptional. The artist's most meaningful works are well represented here. Carl Milles's collection of art from ancient Greece and Rome as well as the European Middle Ages and Renaissance are unique in Sweden and well worth seeing. Temporary exhibitions are arranged throughout the year.

Museum of Modern Art

Birger Jarlsgatan 57. BUS 46.
☎ 08-666 42 50
Open: Tue–Thu 12.00–19.00,
Fri–Sun 12.00–17.00.

The museum's collections are

made up of more than 4000 works by Swedish as well as international artists. Temporary exhibitions are on display in the present museum quarters and the entire collection will be relocated back to Skeppsholmen when the new museum building is completed during the winter of 1997–98.

Museum of Music

Sibyllegatan 2. SUBWAY Östermalmstorg, Kungsträdgården, BUS 62.
☎ 08-666 45 30
Open: Tue–Sun 11.00–16.00.

The museum occupies a 300 year-old former bakery. Instruments, pictures, notes and live music illustrate the role of music at various periods and in various milieux. Special exhibitions include an interactive display, also "Tutti – instruments in time and space" and "Ensembles in Sweden". Many instruments available to be tried by museum visitors. Concerts and children's activities.

National Swedish Museum of Fine Arts

Blasieholmskajen. SUBWAY Kungsträdgården, BUS 65, 62, 46, 76, 59.

☎ 08-666 42 50
Open: Tue 11.00–20.00, Wed–Sun 11.00–17.00.

The museum is in a large building designed in the Venetian, Florentine and Renaissance styles, and is located on Blasieholmen, across the water from the Royal Palace. This is Sweden's largest museum of art, with works from the 15th century to 1900. Paintings by international and Swedish masters, Rembrandt and Renoir, Zorn and Larsson. Famous Swedish paintings are also to be found here, as well as sketches, engravings and crafts, from the Renaissance to modern times. Concerts are held all year round, the most popular of which are summer evening events in the building's grand entrance hall.

Swedish Museum of Natural History

Frescativägen 40. SUBWAY Universitetet, BUS 40, 540.
☎ 08-666 40 00
Open: Daily 10.00–18.00, Thu until 20.00.

Here you will find displays on the polar regions that let you walk into the mouth of a whale, meet penguins and albatrosses and

The magnificent Nordic Museum on a sunny winter's day. Photo: Chad Ehlers/Tiofoto

listen to the calls of the whale and the Weddel seal. Don't miss the exhibit entitled "The Development of the Earth and the Origins of Life" about primordial life forms, dinosaurs, mammoths and early man.

Nordic Museum
Djurgårdsvägen 6–16, BUS 44, 47; also tram and ferry.
☎ 08-666 46 00
Open: Tue–Sun 11.00–17.00, Thu to 20.00.

The largest museum of cultural history in Sweden, the Nordic Museum tells the story of Swedish life and work from the 1500s to the present day. Some 20 exhibitions on various topics, including Swedish guilds, the Sami people of Lappland, folk dress, fashions, Swedish housing and festival and ceremonial traditions over a lifetime. Also, toys from the 1600s to the present, and table settings.

Observatory Museum
Drottninggatan 120. SUBWAY Odenplan.

☎ 08-31 58 10
Open: Guided tours on weekends 12.00, 13.00 and 14.00. Other times shown by arrangement only.

Swedish science and research during the 1700s and 1800s is described, and a focus is given to the works of Pehr Wilhelm Wargentin, the observatory's head and an astronomer who was active through much of the 1700s. In the cellar was the foremost workshop of the day for manufacturing the precision instruments needed for research. One of the largest collections of instruments in Scandinavia is now on display. The museum also has a smaller telescope that is used for group presentations that have been arranged in advance.

Olle Olsson House
Furugatan by Hagalundsgatan 50 in Solna. SUBWAY Solna Centrum, BUS 515.
☎ 08-83 97 44
Open: Wed–Sun 12.00–16.00; 1/7–31/8, weekends 12.00–16.00

The home of artist Olle Olsson is situated in Hagalund's unique cultural surroundings. Inside are works of Olle Olsson Hagalund and his colleagues Hilding Linnqvist, Bror Hjorth, Sven X:et Erixson and others. Films about Olle Olsson are shown continually. Coffee is served in his original kitchen. Gallery with exhibitions of present-day Swedish and international contemporary art.

Police Museum
Polhemsgatan 30. SUBWAY Rådhuset, BUS 40, 48, 62.
☎ 08-401 90 64, 401 90 53 (for bookings)
Open: 15/8–15/6, Tue–Fri by arrangement only (minimum age 18 years).

Stockholm's Police Headquarters houses one of the most interesting police museums in Europe. Collections include a history of police work as well as a review of types of crime and criminal cases in the past and in modern times.

Postal Museum
Lilla Nygatan 6. SUBWAY Gamla Stan, BUS 48, 53.
☎ 08-781 17 55
Open: 1/9–30/4 Tue–Sun 11.00–16.00, Wed to 19.00.

Sweden's only postal history and philatelic museum. The work of the postal service from 1636 until the present day is depicted in a series of living scenes. Stamps and stamp production from 1855 to the present are on display, as are envelopes, postmarks and original artwork for stamp designs. The museum also has collections of Swedish and international rarities and a large library. "Little Post Office" workshop for children.

Prince Eugen's Waldemarsudde
Prins Eugens väg 6, Djurgården. BUS 47.
☎ 08-662 28 00
Open: 1/9–31/5, Tue–Sun 11.00–16.00; 1/6–31/8, Tue and Thu 11.00–20.00, Wed and Fri–Sun 11.00–17.00.

One of Sweden's larger art museums, Waldemarsudde is dedicated primarily to the works of Prince Eugen but also includes collections of Swedish and Nordic artists from the period 1880–1904. The main building includes parts of the Prince's home in their original condition. Large park with gardens and sculpture. Restaurant. Concerts during the summer.

Riddarholm Church
Riddarholmen. SUBWAY Gamla Stan, BUS 48, 53.

☎ 08-402 61 30
Open: 1/6–31/8 daily 12.00–16.00; May and Sep, Wed and weekends 12.00–15.00.

This brick church with its cast-iron spire is on Riddarholmen, the island west of Gamla Stan. The spire is late 19th century, but the building has origins with the Franciscan order back to 1280. Additional changes were made during the 1300s. Riddarholm Church is the chapel and memorial church for Sweden's rulers and other great figures, many of whom are buried there. The interior of the church is adorned with the shields of the Knights of the Order of the Seraphim.

The Swedish Parliament
Riksgatan 3A, Helgeands-holmen. SUBWAY Gamla stan.
☎ 08-789 40 00
Open: The gallery in the Plenary Chamber is open whenever Parliament is in session. In the summer, guided tours 28/6–5/9, Mon–Fri 11.00 (in Swedish), 12.30 (Swedish, English, German), 14.00 (Swe, Eng, in August also French), 15.30 (Swe). In winter, weekends 12.00 (Swe), 13.30 (Swe, Eng).

Visit the Swedish Parliament. Here laws are made, decisions are taken on expenditures and foreign policy is debated. Visitors taking the tour can see the plenary hall, standing committees, a party meeting area and much more in this distinguished turn of the century building.

The Parliament Information Centre on Västerlånggatan (towards Mynttorget) has a permanent exhibition on the Parliament as well as other displays describing Parliamentary activities and history.
Open Sept–May Mon 10.30–17,30, Tue–Fri 9.30–17.30, June–Aug Mon–Fri 9.30–16.30.
☎ 08-786 54 63, -62

The Museum of Swedish Sport
Arenaslingan 5 by Globen. SUBWAY Globen.
☎ 08-600 31 30
Open: 1/9–31/5 Tue–Fri, 12.00–17.00, Thu 12.00–20.00, weekends 11.00–16.00; 1/6–31/8 Tue–Sun 11.00–16.00.

The history of Swedish sport is shown in active displays that include old film and radio. Using computer techniques, visitors can become familiar with Swedish sports figures and even finish their tour with a pentathlon in the activities area.

Rosendal Castle
Rosendalsvagen 41 Djurgården. BUS 47.
☎ 08-402 61 30
Open: 1/6–31/8, Tue–Sun guided tours at 12.00, 13.00, 14.00, 15.00; 1/9–30/9 weekend guided tours at 12.00, 13.00, 14.00, 15.00.

Rosendal Castle, built in 1823–27 for Karl XIV Johan – from plans by Fredrik Blom – has a number of well-preserved interiors that illustrate the Karl-Johan style, the Swedish equivalent of the Empire style.

History of Marine Technology Museum
Djurgårdsbrunnsvägen 24. BUS 69.
☎ 08-666 49 00
Open: Daily 10.00–17.00, in spring and autumn 18.00–20.30.

Swedish shipbuilding, marine defence and commercial shipping from the 17th century to the present. More than 100 models on the same scale portray the growth in size of ships over more than a thousand years. A unique collection of model ships from the 17th and 18th centuries is featured. Original ship interiors, such as from the schooner Hoppets skans (1878), as well as a stern with cabin from Gustav III's schooner Amphion.

Skansen Open-air Museum

Djurgårdsslätten 49–51. BUS 44, 47; tram, ferry.
☎ 08-442 80 00
Open: 1/9–30/4 daily 9.00–16.00; 1/5–31/8 daily 9.00–22.00.
Skansen's houses and farms: 15/9–15/5 daily 11.00–15.00; 16/5–14/9 daily 11.00–17.00.

Skansen is much more than the world's first open-air museum. It is also a place for dancing, entertainment and celebration of the year's festivals. In addition, Skansen is Stockholm's only zoo, with elks, bears, seals and wolves, as well as crocodiles, monkeys, flamingos and other exotic creatures. Stroll among 150 historical buildings – transported here over the years from various regions of Sweden – representing a variety of epochs and social conditions. Crafts and household activities, performed as they would have been in the era depicted, help to make Skansen into a living museum, a "Sweden in miniature".

The Tramway Museum

Tegelviksgatan 22. BUS 46, 66.
☎ 08-686 15 50
Open: Mon–Fri 10.00–17.00, weekends 11.00–16.00.

Visit the Tramway Museum, a fun spot for the entire family. Some 40 vehicles from various periods: horse-drawn buses, trams, motor buses and subway trains reveal the evolution of public transpiration from the 1800s to the present. Visitors are welcome to board our buses and wagons to get a feeling for how things were in the old days. Occasionally guests are even invited to take a riding tour. Library, giftshop and café.

Stockholm City Museum

Ryssgården, Södermalmstorg. SUBWAY Slussen, BUS 43, 46, 48, 53, 55, 59.
☎ 08-700 05 00
Open: 1/9–31/5, Tue–Sun 11.00–17.00, Thu to 21.00; 1/6–31/8, Tue–Sun 11.00–17.00, Thu to 19.00.

Interested in the history of Stockholm? Visit the City Museum and browse among a wide variety of exhibitions: the Stockholm region in the Iron Age; trade and craft in the 17th century; the Tre

Kronor Fort and the Lohe treasure; Liberty; Gustav III's proud city; life in the industrial city of the 1890s; Stockholm's development in maps and pictures; topographical art in Stockholm.

The Strindberg Museum, Blue Tower

Drottningatan 85. SUBWAY Rådmansgatan, BUS 40, 53, 69, 52.
☎ 08-411 53 54
Open: Tue 11.00–19.00, Wed–Fri 11.00–16.00, weekends 12.00–16.00.

The last place where Sweden's best-known writer, August Strindberg, lived. His library is kept here. Basic exhibitions about Strindberg's life, times and writing. Talks, discussions and theatre performances. Temporary exhibitions.

The National Swedish Museum of Science and Technology

Museivägen 7, Norra Djurgården. BUS 69.
☎ 08-663 10 85, 5789 000–2328 # (24 hours)
Open: Mon–Fri 10.00–16.00, weekends 12.00–16.00.

The museum highlights developments in technology, industry, engineering and natural history. Various departments focus on mining technology, steam machinery, automobiles, bicycles, home making, chemistry, electricity, printing, forest industries and construction. The Mine and Machine Hall has been renovated. Certain areas are closed for renovation and will reopen autumn 1997.

"Teknorama" is Sweden's first Science Centre. Here you will find more than 100 experiment stations. An exhibit entitled Discover, Explore and Experience contains experiments in technology and biology. A kaleidoscope of technical history starts in ancient times and reaches to the future.

The Telecommunications Museum

Museivägen 7, Norra Djurgården, BUS 69.
☎ 08-670 81 00, Internet: http://www.telemuseum.se
Open: Mon–Fri 10.00–16.00, weekends 12.00–16.00.

Here you'll find the entire history of telecommunications, from signal fires to the Internet! In addition to permanent exhibits describing telegraphy, telephony, radio and television there is also a manned amateur radio station and news editing room for school groups. Another room is dedicated to the memory of L.M. Ericsson, Sweden's telephone industry pioneer.

The Thiel Art Gallery

Sjötullsbacken 6, Djurgården. BUS 69.
☎ 08-662 58 84
Open: Mon–Sat 12.00–16.00, Sun 13.00–16.00.

When, at the end of the last century, banker Ernest Thiel could no longer find room for all his paintings in his Strandvägen apartment, he had a grand house built on Djurgården. His guests included people like Verner von Heidenstam, Ellen Key, Bruno Liljefors, Carl Larsson, Hugo Alfvén and Hjalmar Söderberg. In 1924 the gallery was made available to the public. The original milieu, well preserved, offers a unique collection of Nordic art, including Edvard Munch, Zorn, Liljefors and Carl Larsson.

Tobaksmuseet (The Tobacco Museum)

Gubbhyllan, Skansen. BUS 44, 47; tram, ferry.

☎ 08-442 80 26
Open: 1/5–17/9, daily 11.00–17.00; 18/9–30/4, daily 11.00–15.00; handcraft Sundays 11.00–16.00.

The Tobacco Museum concentrates mainly on the history of tobacco in Sweden, from the early 17th century onwards. Exhibits on four floors include a series of moist-snuff tins and boxes, pipes, cigar racks and cutters, cigarette boxes and packets, posters and advertising, lighters etc.

Tom Tit's Experiment

Storgatan 33, RAIL Södertälje C.
☎ 08-550 190 44, Internet: http://www.tomtit.se
Open: daily 10.00–18.00, Thu also to 21.00, 24/6–11/8 daily 10.00–18.00.

Tom Tit's Experiment lets visitors of all ages experiment with sound, light, water, air, motion and other phenomenon. A special section is dedicated to the human body. A new addition is available with displays adapted for visitors with different handicaps.

Torekällsberget Museum

Torekällberget, Södertälje. RAIL Södertälje C.
☎ 08-550 214 22

Open: Winter daily 11.00–15.00, Summer daily 11.00–16.00, Wed 11.00–19.00.

Open museum of cultural history, with buildings from old Södertälje and the surrounding countryside. "The country" with large farms, crofts, and Swedish livestock, culture, historic play cottage and school. "The city" with apartment houses, crafts, people and shops.

Tullgarn Castle
Tullgarn. RAIL to Södertälje Hamn, then by BUS to Tullgarns allé.
☎ 08-551 720 11
Open: Guided tours May–Sep, 11.00–16.00 on the hour.

Tullgarn Castle is famous as the castle that Gustav V used in the summer. It became a Royal out-of-town residence in 1722. Visit the well-preserved apartment of Duke Fredrik Adolf and Queen Viktoria's breakfast room, in the South German Renaissance style. Splendid parks. Tullgarn's Inn.

Submarine "Minken"
Wasahamnen, Djurgården. BUS 44, 47, tram, ferry.
☎ 070-787 72 80
Open: May–Sept daily 10.00–20.00, Oct–April weekends 10.00–17.00.

U105,9 is a genuine submarine from the Soviet era, now moored alongside the Vasa Museum. Curious visitors can go on aboard and experience the cramped quarters and imagine the difficult living conditions. "Minken" is the last boat in the long line of "Whiskey" class submarines as they were termed by Nato forces.

Ulriksdal Castle
Bergshamra, Solna. SUBWAY Bergshamra, then BUS 540.
☎ 08-85 05 56
Open: Spring and autumn, weekends 12.00–16.00; summer, Tue–Sun 12.00–16.00.

Ulriksdal Castle dates from the 17th century, the era when Sweden was a major regional power. At the castle is the richly embroidered coronation carriage (1650) of Queen Kristina, as well as an orangery from the turn of the 18th century, with trees and plants from around the Mediterranean and sculptures from Sweden (1700–1900).

The Vasa Museum
Galärvarvet, Djurgården. BUS 44, 47; tram, ferry.
☎ 08-666 48 00

The Vasa Museum is Sweden's most popular tourist attraction. Photo: Hans Hammarskiöld/Stockholm Information Service

Open: 10/6–20/8, daily 9.30–19.00; 21/8–9/6 daily 10.00–17.00, Wed to 20.00.

One of Sweden's biggest tourist attractions. The man-of-war Vasa sank in the port of Stockholm on its maiden voyage in 1628. More than three centuries later, in 1961, the ship was raised, restored and is now on show as the only ship in the world remaining from the 17th century. Even the setting for the ship inspires awe; it may be viewed and inspected from six different levels, at a distance and at close quarters. A scale model, seven metres long, represents the Vasa before it sank, and the museum has several other exhibits regarding the ship.

Museum ships Sankt Erik and Finngrundet

Open: 10/6–20/8, daily 12.00–17.00; 21/8–9/6, weekends 12.00–17.00.

Moored outside the museum are the ice breaker Sankt Erik and the lightship Finngrundet. Built in 1915, S.S. Sankt Erik was Sweden's first ice breaker, and it remained in active service until 1977. The Finngrundet lightship was built in 1903 and was in service until 1969.

Vaxholm Fort Museum

Vaxholm Citadel. Boat to Vaxholm, or BUS 670 from SUBWAY Tekniska Högskolan.
☎ 08-541 720 00, 541 721 57
Open: 15/5–31/8 daily 12.00–15.45; other times by arrangement.

Visit Vaxholm and it's citadel. Like many forts, it was out of date before it was completed. The reason here was the ribbed cannonball, which proved easily capable of breaking the building's walls apart. The fort now serves as a museum, with displays of artillery equipment from the past, as well as exhibits about the history of the defence of the archipelago from 1500 to 1900.

The Wine and Distillery Museum

Dalagatan 100. SUBWAY Odenplan.
☎ 08-744 70 70
Open: Tue 10.00–19.00, Wed–Fri 10.00–16.00, weekends 12.00–16.00.

The museum traces the history of wine, punch and Swedish snaps – all in fascinating surroundings. Look into a wine shop and a Skåne potato distillery from the turn of the century. Test your sense of smell by identifying some of the 55 snaps spices in our "scent organ"!

The Museum of Far Eastern Antiquities

Tyghusplan, Skeppsholmen. SUBWAY Kungsträdgården, BUS 65.
☎ 08-666 42 50
Open: Tue 12.00–20.00, Wed–Sun 12.00–17.00.

The museum occupies a long, narrow building – once quarters for Karl II's bodyguards. On display are collections of fine art objects from China, Japan, Korea and India, from the Stone Age to the late 19th century, including one of the world's most eminent collections of Chinese art outside Asia.

EVERY YEAR
IN STOCKHOLM

*The Stockholm Water Festival
is the really big annual event. For ten days
at the beginning of August, Stockholm explodes
in fireworks, street life and parties. Altogether
there are some 1000 events.*

You can buy a Vattenpass (water pass), which serves as an admissions ticket and gives reduced prices for dozens of restaurants, pubs, shops and travel for the whole of the summer. The profit made from the festival and the water pass goes to the Stockholm Water Prize, a one-million Kronor environment prize awarded annually to an outstanding researcher in the field of water conservation.

Stockholm has a lot more to offer. Here is a calendar of annual events. Note, however, that scheduling times can vary from year to year.

January

Aktivaden

Sport and activities exhibition at the Stockholm International Fairs. Try different sports!

Walt Disney on Ice

Disney's well-known characters in an ice show at Globen Arena.

Husdjursmässan

Pet and domestic animal exhibition at Sollentuna exhibition hall.

February

Vårsalongen

Spring salon at Liljevalch's art

The Stockholm Water Festival in early August raises the spirits of both locals and visitors. Every other evening features a glittering fireworks display. Photo: Claes Löfgren/Pressens Bild

The Stockholm Art Fair is an international art exhibition held each year in Sollentuna. Photo: Pelle Stackman/Tiofoto

gallery on Djurgården. After selection from among thousands of contributors, nonestablished artists are given a chance to show their work at one of the city's most reputed art galleries. The exhibition goes on from February until the end of March.

Sweden Hockey Games.
International ice-hockey competition at Globen arena.

DN Games.
Track and field competition with international participants. Globen.

March

Allt för Sjön
(Boat show) The Nordic region's largest boat show, with everything for the motoring or sailing yachter. Stockholm International Fairs.

Stockholm Art Fair.
International art fair with emphasis on Swedish work. Sollentuna exhibition hall.

April

Wilderness Expo
Sport fishing, hunting, camping and travel. Sollentuna exhibition hall.

The Circus Princess.
Top international women circus performers gather to compete for the title of Circus Princess.

Antique Exhibition
Art, interiors and design of the highest quality. Stockholm International Fairs.

Gröna Lund
Stockholm's amusement park is opened for the season.

Valborg's Eve.
Celebrated nationally with bonfires, fireworks and spring songs. Yearly gathering at Skansen.

May

Hat Parade
From the Nordic Museum to Skansen. Hats of all colours, shapes and sizes.

Tjejtrampet
("girl's pedal") World's largest bicycle event with approximately 9000 female entrants of all ages. Party on Gärdet with entertainment and presentation of prizes.

Drakfesten
Kite flying, Gärdet. The art school organises this event, and Gärdet is full of enthusiasts with flying objects of every imaginable form. North Djurgården.

Elitloppet
Elite Series at Solvalla. Trotters race in the most prestigious competition of the year at the county's largest track.

Restaurant Day
Some 35 of Stockholm's restaurants are on display, offering food and drink over a three-day period in Kungsträdgården. Many visitors in a pleasant setting.

June

Stockholm marathon
The race goes twice round the city, starting at Östermalm's sports ground at Lidingövägen at 15.00, finishing at Stadion. About 13,000 participants from 30 countries make it one of the world's largest marathons.

Skärgårdsbåtens dag
(Archipelago boat day) A cavalcade of steam boats across the water from Stockholm to Vaxholm and back to Strömkajen. Party at Vaxholm with fried

The Stockholm Marathon is one of the world's largest. Photo: Martin Ceije/Pressens Bild

herring, lottery, chocolate wheels, music, dancing etc. Vaxholm and Stockholm.

Sweden's national day and Swedish Flag day
Celebrated 6 June, mainly at Skansen.

Olympic Day Run
Untimed run around Riddar-fjärden. Open to all. Run with athletes from 150 countries.

Stockholm's Orient Festival
Features Arabic culture in Gälarparken on Djurgården. International culture festival.

Music at the Palace
Classical concerts in royal surroundings with Swedish and foreign artists.

Stockholm Games GP
International track and field events at Stockholm stadium.

Midsummer celebrations
with fiddle music, dancing, raising of the midsummer pole, at Skansen and other locations.

Gotland Runt
(Around Gotland) One of the world's largest sailing races in terms of number of boats. About

450 boats depart from Sandhamn for a few days' sailing round Gotland and back. Saturday is perhaps the best day to experience the boats and the crowd. Sandhamn, outer archipelago.

July

Stockholm Summer Games
International youth competition in numerous events at various arenas in Stockholm.

Asian Festival
A cultural experience with art and cuisine from Asian nations.

Skansen Jazz and Blues Festival
Not only jazz and blues but also rock and gospel by well-known performers from far and wide.

DN-Galan
International track and field. Sweden's best arena competition and one of the world's 15 Grand Prix competitions. Stadion, Stockholm.

Skoklosterspelen
Historical family festival including jousting, acting, music and various artists at Skokloster.

Bellman Festival
Numerous programmes all over Stockholm to honour the memory of the 18th-century poet Carl Michael Bellman. The most ceremonious and also the most fun is usually on Bellman's Day at the end of July.

During July many large, outdoor concerts are arranged with popular singers and ensambles.

August

Stockholm Water Festival
The city's largest happening with a variety of events concentrated around Gustav Adolf Square, Norrbro, Riddarholmen and the quays. Opera, concerts and other events. Theatre. Sporting events. Exhibitions. International fireworks competition over several evenings. Awarding of the year's Stockholm Water Prize for work in the field of water conservation.

Midnattsloppet
One of Söder's big parties, where thousands of joggers run through the August night. Part of Stockholm Water Festival.

Roslagsloppet

Motorboat competition starting at Strömmen in Stockholm, finish at Öregrund in Roslagen.

Stockholm Gospel Choir Festival

On Sergels Torg and other locations throughout the city.

Symphony on the Green

Outdoor concert at the Maritime Museum on Gärdet. A delightful festival with an enormous audience.

Strindberg Festival in Stockholm.

Cultural event with prose, theatre and exhibitions surrounding the writer August Strindberg's life and works.

Portrait of August Strindberg (1896) Photo: Pressens Bild

Tjejmilen

About 30,000 women run, jog or walk over a ten-kilometre stretch of Djurgården. The competition is one of the largest of its kind in the world.

Each August the public is invited to an open-air concert at the History of Marine Technology Museum. Photo: Sam Stadener/Pressens Bild

September

Segelbåtens Dag
(Sailboat Day) Races around most stretches of water in Stockholm and the surrounding area. Certain events feature classic wooden boats.

Bellman Relay
Sweden's largest relay race starting and finishing in Stora Skuggan by Frescati Park.

Stockholm Beer Festival
More than 340 varieties of beer, a food-and-beer school, seminars and entertainment. Nacka Strand exhibition hall and Congress Centre in Nacka.

October

Lidingöloppet
Largest cross-country running race in the world. Thirty kilometres and 15 kilometres, respectively. Elite and amateur runners. Last day of enrolment is six weeks before the competition. Lidingö.

November

Stockholm Open
Top professionals compete at the Royal Tennis Hall.

Stockholm FilmFestival
Ten days of films, seminars, actors and awards for best films.

Segelbåtens Dag (Sailboat Day). Photo: Max Ström/Pressens Bild

The 18-year old French horseman Lorenzo, alias Laurent Serré, captivates the public with his white chargers at Globen arena. Anders Kallersand/ Pressens Bild

Stockholm Globe Arena International Horse Show

World Cup competition in dressage and show jumping.

December

Skansen's Christmas Fair

Sales of arts and crafts, Christmas

Christmas market on Stortorget in Gamla Stan. Photo: Ingemar Aourell/ Stockholm Information Service

decorations, home-made candles, bread, cakes etc. Sausages grilled over open fires. Christmas table prepared in some of the historic buildings. Sundays 11.00–16.00. Skansen. Christmas markets are arranged at numerous spots in the greater Stockholm area.

Nobeldagen

(Nobel Day) Year's Nobel Prizes awarded 10 December by H M King Carl XVI Gustaf at a formal ceremony in the Concert House, Stockholm. Only invited guests. Banquet at City Hall in the evening.

Lucia

Celebrations throughout Stockholm. Coronation of the year's "Lucia" at Skansen.

New Year's celebration

Fireworks all over the city. New Year celebration at Skansen with reading of "New Year Bells", broadcast direct on TV.

TRIPS, OUTDOOR ACTIVITIES AND SPORTS

The areas surrounding Stockholm are just as fascinating as the city itself and well worth visiting. To the east lies the archipelago with its thousands of islands, small villages, summer cottages and nature reserves. To the west around Lake Mälaren, one can find interesting small towns, farm country and manor houses.

It is almost always possible to reach the areas described throughout this book by boat, bus or local train. For more information, contact one of the tourist bureaux or call the information number for public transportation ☎ 08-600 10 00). Individuals or groups interested in package tours and related information should contact Utflyktsbutiken for booking and information. Utflyktsbutiken is situated in Sverigehuset (Sweden House) på Hamngatan 27, ☎ 08-789 24 15.

The archipelago village of Berg on Möja.

Travelling to Vaxholm is a highly popular day trip, particularly on Archipelago Boats Day. Photos: Jeppe Wikström/Pressens Bild

121

*One of Stockholm's great advantages
is its successful contrasting of open landscape and modern
cityscape. This varied combination offers enormous possibilities
for outdoor activities, sports and exercise for local residents
and visitors alike.*

Cycling

The city's complete network of bicycle paths makes cycling safe and pleasant. Few cities in the world are so well adapted for cycling and it is arguably the best way to get around the Stockholm area and even the surrounding countryside. Head for a cultural landmark or the open country. You'll need some good maps and always use a helmet. Look out for pedestrians on the cycle paths, they are often in the way. Stockholm has many bicycle rental shops and these can be found in the yellow pages of the telephone directory under Cyklar – Uthyrning.

Fishing

It's true that you can catch large salmon in the middle of the city. You can also angle for perch and pike in one of the lakes or well out into the Baltic. Get a fishing license if you plan to go angling on the smaller inland waters. Fishing is free in the archipelago, Lake Mälaren and Stockholm's Stream as long as one uses a rod, hook and line or other hand gear. You can fish from shore or boat, but always check your rights and responsibilities according to "Allemansrätten" – Sweden's right of public access*. Note: Fishing can be limited or forbidden in certain nature reserves, nesting areas, and military protection areas. Check the regulations for specific locations. Regulations regarding types of equipment used also apply to non-citizens.

Outdoor activities

On sparkling winter days you'll find plenty of people at Hellasgården, Lida or one of the other classic nature parks around the city. The metro-

Lida, one of Stockholm's parks on a sunny day in winter. Photo: Hans Nelsäter/Bildarkivet

politan area has some 30 such reserves and all of them are wonderful destinations for the whole family. Most of these areas feature jogging tracks and trails for hiking and cross-country skiing. Often visitors also have access to showers, saunas and restaurants. Most of these parks are easily reachable using public transport and parking is available for those travelling by car.

Jogging

A leading American magazine described Stockholm as the world's most beautiful city for runners. Metropolitan joggers will have no difficulty finding running areas near the water where the asphalt changes to gravel and even woodland paths – all within the city limits. Just outside the city, jogging opportunities are virtually unlimited. The county's townships offer many dedicated tracks and trails, often with lighting.

Paddling

Paddling can make for a relaxing or a strenuous adventure. Choose the experience you're looking for; a calm evening on a mirror-smooth lake, a tour along marked "trails" in rural waters, island hopping in the archipelago, or open-water work in the Baltic.

Hiking

Few large cities can boast Stockholm's proximity to natural environments. Ten minutes travel by underground from downtown to Björkhagen station will land you in the Nacka reserve and its entrance onto the Sörmland hiking trail (Sörmlandsleden). If you want to hike Roslagsleden to Norrtälje you can start in Danderyd just north of Stockholm. Another fine trail is Upplandsleden, which starts in Barkarby, one of the western suburbs. Most of these "leder" are equally well-suited for day trips or extended overnight journeys. Don't forget your canteen!

Berry and produce picking

Pack a picnic basket with some good things and head out to pick some berries and vegetables. This type of outing is a great way to experience the countryside and the farmers can provide you with good tips about local swimming spots or worthwhile sights. Note: Try to call growers in advance to check on open times and directions. Growers offering pick-it-yourself crops often advertise in the newspapers and post signs outside their farms.

Skating

Taking a long-distance skating tour is the height of Nordic exoticism for many visitors. After such a trip it's easy to understand the fascination of this sport and how it keeps the "old-timers" skating from the first solid freeze in winter until the spring thaw. Lake Mälaren, the inland lakes and the archipelago all offer unique skating experiences in the right weather. Many lakes are plowed to create long tracks, thus providing the local populace with a new gathering place come winter. Ice rinks and man-made tracks are also common alternatives for willing skaters.

A Sunday stroll on the ice. Photo: Hans Nelsäter/Bildarkivet

Note: Avoid skating alone, particularly in areas far from help. Experienced skaters on long trips travel in a group with safety equipment and a change of clothes. Ask for more information at sporting goods stores.

Skiing

Stockholmers are avid skiers. When the real snow and cold arrives the larger parks and nature reserves are excellent destinations near to hand. Djurgården is the most central spot for skiing in the city and adjacent areas offer hundreds of kilometres of trails from which to choose. Downhill skiers have a number of small, local hills to help maintain their style and form. Two of the most popular are Hammarbybacken in southern Stockholm with its excellent view of the city and Flottsbro in the town of Huddinge. With some cooperation from the weather and regular snow making these hills can be skied from December to April.

* For more information about "Allemansrätten" Sweden's right of public access see the Practical Information section of this book, contact a tourist bureau or call Naturvårdsverket (☎ 08-698 10 00).